"Goot for You!"

The Laughable Life of
a Second Wife

KERRY KENDALL

NDYGIRLS PUBLISHING
POINCIANA, FLORIDA

Editor: Nicole K. Rossi

Back Cover Photo:
Debbie Mitts Photography

Library of Congress Control Number: 2012943117
NDYGirls Publishing, Poinciana, FL

ISBN-13: 978-0615661124
ISBN-10: 0615661122
Printed in the United States.

Dedication

This book is dedicated to Dr. Tarique Perera, the very nice psychiatrist in Connecticut, who kept me calm and medicated during my first few years of marriage. During our sessions, he politely suppressed most of his laughter while I described, in great detail, the events of my life as David's second wife.

I remember the day he increased the dosage of my medication and gave me a warning.

> Dr. P.: I want you to be aware of any changes in your mental health that might lead to changes in your behavior.
>
> Kerry: Like what?
>
> Dr. P.: You need to call me right away if you should feel suicidal.
>
> Kerry: I never feel suicidal, only homicidal.
>
> Dr. P.: In your case, that's healthy.

Really, that's exactly what he said.

The medication worked well. My vivid dreams of revenge were enough to keep me from actually buying a gun. But I do have a few hit-and-run plans sketched out on cocktail napkins that I keep filed away in a safe place, just in case. You never know. Something might push me over the edge. In the meantime, I walk among you, appearing as normal as anyone, thanks to Dr. Perera.

That historic day when Dr. Perera said, "Goot for you!" ("Good for You!" with a slight Indian accent), I knew I had the tools to survive all the enabling and dysfunction.

Contents

"Goot for You!"

Disclaimer

This book is not intended to take the place of sound advice from a medical professional or a professional bartender. Neither the author nor the publisher assumes any liability for adverse consequences resulting from following in the footsteps of any of the characters in this book.

The names of the characters in this book have been changed for almost the same reason the old *Dragnet* t.v. series didn't use real names: "to protect the innocent." However, in this case, the names have been changed to protect the guilty. The dysfunctional characteristics and actions of the feckless people in the author's real life have been either melded together or separated, in most cases, in order to create a new character who is just as fucked-up as the original.

The character of the author, however, will be played by herself, using her real name and real feelings at all times.

Please don't feel cheated by this disclaimer. You don't need to read between the lines. It's all there with just a little tweaking. Currently it's called "narrative non-fiction." It used to be called "the new journalism." You know, like Carl Bernstein's *All the President's Men* or Tom Wolfe's *The Right Stuff.* It could also be called "a true story from one person's point-of-view, told with enough subjective detail so that you can feel the pain and hear the laughter."

The events are not in chronological order.

Acknowledgments

I have a wonderful husband who admits he likes my writing despite the subjects I write about and the embarrassing stories that are told at his expense. He knows his *baggage* has put me through the wringer and he tries to compensate for that by leaving me alone with my laptop for long periods of time.

My friend Julie tried to prevent me from embarking on the journey that resulted in this book. But when she couldn't, she stayed the course with me. She's helped me to cope in the eye of the storm. I'd like to think I helped her from time to time too.

My sounding boards over the past 17 years of my life with David have been Joyce, Gigi, Rosanne and Lisa, among others. Thanks girls. Your friendships have been invaluable in keeping my head above water and out of the noose.

The *Sisterhood of SolWriters* at Solivita ("that evil writers' group," according to David) has been encouraging, critical and demanding in seeing this project get finished. And the *Not Dead Yet Girls, Serious Authors, Comic Relief,* are living the publishing dream with me. Girlfriends are the best friends.

My editor, Nicole Rossi, who says her brain came out with her placenta upon the births of both her boys, is still smart enough to keep the printed words in order and in the correct tense while laughing. I'm hoping her book club likes our work too.

And finally, I need to acknowledge my network. I keep in touch with a lot of people. It's the reporter in me. I'm genuinely interested in what happens to people over the course of their lives. Maybe one of them will let me write their story next. But for now, I thank them for getting the word out about mine.

Prologue

My friend Julie married a very successful businessman who is financially secure and the divorced father of three daughters whom she thought might become her friends someday, or at the very least, a tolerable family around the holidays. It didn't happen.

Years later, I started dating David, also a successful businessman who is financially secure and the divorced father of two boys and a girl. When I told Julie, she said, "Get out now!" I didn't. She repeated it. I still didn't listen. Three years later, I married David. Not long after, I wished I had listened to Julie.

Later still, my friend Leslie started dating Ron, a guy with a lot of potential and wonderful qualities who treats her well. He's the divorced father of three boys. When she told me that little tidbit of information, I begged her, "Get out now!" She didn't. I wasn't persuasive enough. I didn't give her all the play-by-play that Julie and I had shared over the years. But thank goodness we took notes.

These are the *real* stories about the *real* stepchildren and ex-wives, mostly mine, some Julie's. But she's writing her own book (the working title is *Bundle of Joy, My Ass!*), so I won't repeat all of her stories. Besides, both of our lives would overwhelm most women who don't work in the field of mental healthcare or in the federal prison system.

Remarkably, both Julie and I have stayed married. I'm sure it helped that we were both struggling with similar issues at different times. We had each other to vent to. And now you have us, or at least our tales of adventure, which will give you plenty of opportunity to look at your own life and say, "Hey, it could be worse." It was for us.

The Family Trees of
Kerry and Julie

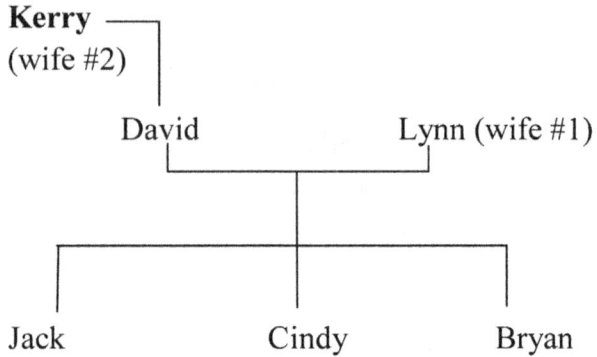

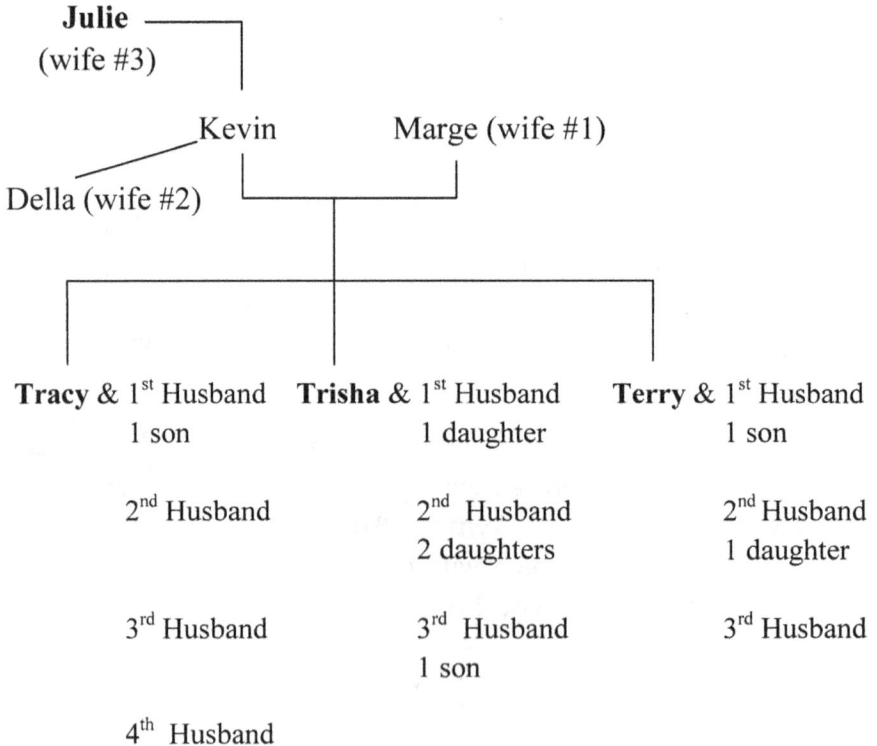

Kerry ——┐
(wife #2)   │

David   Lynn (wife #1)

Jack   Cindy   Bryan

Julie ——┐
(wife #3)

Kevin   Marge (wife #1)

Della (wife #2)

Tracy & 1ˢᵗ Husband	**Trisha** & 1ˢᵗ Husband	**Terry** & 1ˢᵗ Husband
1 son	1 daughter	1 son
2ⁿᵈ Husband	2ⁿᵈ Husband	2ⁿᵈ Husband
	2 daughters	1 daughter
3ʳᵈ Husband	3ʳᵈ Husband	3ʳᵈ Husband
	1 son	
4ᵗʰ Husband		

1

Me, Julie & the Crown

Julie came to Jackson, Mississippi about two years after I did. Same reason. We were both looking to further our careers in television news and Jackson is a pretty good place to do that. It isn't big enough to break you if you're awful, yet it's big enough to launch you if you stand out from the crowd. She's from Missouri and I'm from Connecticut.

I covered sports. Not exactly what you'd expect to find in the Deep South: a white, female, *Yankee* sportscaster. Somehow, I actually fit in. It's the most fun job I can imagine for anyone in their 20s, any gender or race. Watch the game, talk to the players, be on television. But after you grow up and out of your 20s, you've either got to love it or leave it. I didn't love it enough and I left the business after 12 years.

Julie did news, and weather when she was forced to, like when the weatherman called in sick. Those were some of the greatest shows. Not quite a meteorologist, she always seemed to forecast a 50% chance of sun and a 50% chance of rain. She was right most of the time. She lasted in the business much longer than I did, but eventually left for greener pastures and life out of the public eye.

It's easy to bond with your co-workers when you're all far away from home, young and single. They become your family. We had a lively group in Jackson and most of us keep in touch.

Julie was a godsend to me when my sports director and I got fired not long after she came to town. The station had just changed management and hired a news director *of color* and they replaced the pale sports director and me with sportscasters *of color*. Jackson, Mississippi hasn't changed as much as most people would think.

The comfort of having a friend like Julie is probably what made me stay there for another year. Unlike my place, her apartment was so homey. Her parents had helped her move in and they drove all her furniture and things from home in Missouri. I came to town with two suitcases and no flair for decorating.

While together in Jackson, we both remained single and spent lots of time by the pool at my place or at the minor league ballpark, where I was always welcome even after being fired. Or at the mall, doing what we do best, shopping! She taught me how to shop with a purpose. Whenever she broke up with someone she was dating, she shopped for something special to commemorate the occasion. She even bought a tree once. And you should see the $400 Fuck-Johnny! purse. Gorgeous! I was inspired and started buying jewelry for each of my errors in judgment. My favorite is the Fuck-Ben! ring. It didn't cost much, but it's the thought that counts. And I was thinking plenty when I bought it.

We were often impulse shoppers, like the time we left my pool in our bikinis and cover-ups and headed straight for a car dealership. I don't remember if there was a break up involved or if Julie was just tired of her old Datsun 280Z. There we were on the lot, looking beachy, and not one salesman paid attention. I guess they thought we didn't look like buyers. After a while, one lucky young guy finally came up to us.

Julie pointed at a Nissan Altima and said, "I'll take that one."

Initially he was thrilled, until he had to negotiate with me. I see car buying as a team sport.

As soon as we got the car for much lower than the sticker price, we knew we had to break it in on a little road trip. We drove to Shreveport, Louisiana. The Jackson Mets double-A baseball team, with players around our age, were on the road to play the Shreveport Captains that weekend. There just happened to be a vacancy at the team's hotel. Neither of us had ever been to Shreveport before and we've never gone back. The humidity was a killer. It must have been over 100 degrees at the ballpark for the damn doubleheader. We should have done a better job of checking the schedule because even I didn't want to watch a doubleheader in Louisiana in July. Thank God it was nice and cool in the bars and clubs we went to afterward.

That weekend, the Mets manager, Sam Perlozzo, and the team's radio broadcaster, Bill Wahlberg, actually taught Julie how to keep score in an authentic baseball scorebook. Really. It was a very innocent weekend. Booze and baseball and scoring in a book, but nothing else. We just wanted an on-the-road adventure with the new car.

This was five years before *Thelma and Louise* hit the big screen. We hadn't experienced depressive episodes or desperation yet. However, now we find that movie inspiring and their road trip looks pretty good. Even the ending. We didn't have a clue at the time, but there would be plenty of days ahead when both of us would have liked to hit the gas and driven off a cliff to get away from the madness we would marry into.

Funny coincidence: Billy Beane was with the Jackson Mets that season. And Brad Pitt, who became a star after appearing in *Thelma and Louise*, was nominated for an Academy Award for his portrayal of Billy Beane in the movie *Moneyball*. Not a big deal to you, but hey, Julie and I are two degrees of separation from Brad Pitt. By the way, Julie is also two degrees of separation from Kevin Bacon, but I digress.

Although Julie and I came from very different backgrounds (me, blue collar, and her, white collar), we were kind of at the same place in our lives. Neither one of us has a sister and it was nice to be able to share things with someone who understood. Both of us also love animals. People who love animals are just better people in general, if you ask me. They, the people, as well as the animals, make great friends because they care. They even care enough to warn us to get out of a relationship they know will lead to plenty of chaos and heartache. If we don't listen, well, that's our own damn fault.

During our t.v. careers, our dating, shopping, whatever, we were never competitive. Not until we got married to the enabling men with the dysfunctional children. Then the tragic/comedic competition began, and unfortunately, it has never ended.

It started off as a joke when I told Julie I'd win "the crown" if one of David's kids did *fill-in-the-blank* before Kevin's kids. She'd come back at me with a victory and possession of "the crown" if one of Kevin's kids did something even more stupid. Although "the crown" is merely figurative, it's got a lot of mileage on it and it's still traveling between us almost 20 years later.

The holiday weekends are always the best. We can count on some shit hitting the fan when the kids get together with each other or their mothers. Involvement with dad is inevitable after the initial disaster, and then it hits us. Smack in the face. Then we have something else to deal with that should have been dealt with long ago if someone with parenting skills had a clue. It's the absence of those skills that fuel every fire we have to put out in our marriages. Well, that coupled with the money that David and Kevin keep doling out to their kids. They've been given cars and apartments, sent to psychologists and detox centers, and bailed out of jail, yet they still feel entitled to ask for more rather than getting an education, earning a living, or doing something for themselves.

As of this writing, Kevin's girls are in their late 40s and David's two oldest are in their 30s, the youngest is 25. That's an awfully long time to be dependent financially and emotionally. It's also a very long time for Julie and me to be watching the messes unfold. If we didn't have each other, I don't think either of us would still be married.

Looking at each of our lives individually, you would definitely find justification for us to leave our husbands on their own to clean up after themselves and their children. But when you take our lives together, as we've learned to do, this can-you-top-this-train-wreck competition is quite a show. It's hard to look away. We've got to stick around to see who wins and who, among the mutant offspring and enabling fathers, is left standing. There's got to be an end to this game, right?

There was an end for Tracy, Kevin's oldest. She committed suicide at age 47 by taking an overdose of drugs prescribed by her psychiatrist.

We haven't experienced a suicide yet, but it won't surprise me. Nothing will. I'm beyond surprise.

2

Advice

You're probably wondering why I didn't take Julie's advice years ago and "Get out now!" So am I. I've thought about it many times and the only thing I can say in my defense is that somewhere, deep down inside of me, I didn't think she was serious. I met David when I was 34, an age when my *fling* days were over. I was thinking long-term and Julie knew it. She couldn't possibly be telling me to cast this wonderful guy aside just because he had three kids. From the stories she told me over the past few years of her marriage, I knew David's kids could never be as bad as Kevin's kids. Her stories were bizarre. I didn't think she made that stuff up, but really. What were the chances that we'd be able to start a competition as to whose stepchildren were the worst? Best maybe, but worst? It was such a long shot that I didn't even consider the possibility.

Fast forward 17 years to the following email exchange:

Dear Julie,

David just got a call and said, "Dear God!" I can't wait to get the details on this one. Will it ever end?

Kerry

Dear Kerry,

No, it won't ever end. Kevin said the other day that he feels bad about his kids not speaking to him, but it was sure nice not having to listen to all the bullshit.

Julie

Except for Julie's stepdaughters, all the other young Southern women I had met were hard-working, ambitious, talented and smart. Of course all the other young Southern women I had met were somehow connected to my television career. They were either scholar athletes themselves, or the friends or relatives of up-and-coming amateur or professional athletes. And if I didn't see them in their school setting, it was on the courts or the links of one of the many country clubs in the Jackson area. They always looked fashionably feminine with full make-up and perfect hair, like they were biding their time between pageants and just had a moment or two to fit me in for an interview.

Maybe it was the distance that had me fooled into believing my stepkids would be different. Mississippi and Connecticut are miles apart in culture too. And everybody knows the difference in per capita income in those states. David and I even lived in Fairfield County, the richest county in Connecticut. That's where we both grew up. My friends and I were all top-notch students who had the advantage of terrific public schools. We went on to wonderful careers. Three girls in my high school class went on to become medical doctors. I don't think anyone in my graduating class ever delivered a pizza unless the purpose was to gather intel en route to becoming a district manager.

I knew it was different in the South, or at least I had heard it was. Lots of people sent their children to private or religious schools in Mississippi. Kevin's girls went to public schools. Julie might be seeing the result of a lack of education. Perhaps the girls weren't stupid, just undereducated. Everyone can learn, maybe it was just taking them more time to catch up with the Northerners.

Fast forward just two years into my relationship with David, the following conversation:

David: Jack's not graduating from high school.
Kerry (now a high school teacher): Why not?

David: His guidance counselor made a mistake and he didn't take enough history classes.

Kerry: Oh.

It actually hurt for me not to comment any further. Jack went to Staples High School in Westport, the kind of place that would not have an incompetent guidance counselor. This was the first time I realized that either David wasn't as smart as I thought he was, or he was taking a detour into the Land of Denial so he wouldn't have to incur the shame of turning out a non-graduate in Westport, Connecticut.

Although Julie's advice to leave David did not fall on deaf ears, something made me stay to face the challenges ahead. They say love is blind. Maybe I was in my own Land of Denial, but I didn't think I'd end up in the *exact same* situation as Julie. It was too absurd to imagine.

Over the years I don't know how she and I endured, forced to watch parents perpetuating a cycle of boorish behavior. I still don't. By the time you get to the end of this book, that's what many of you will be wondering about both of us. When you get there, I hope to have an answer for you. I want to prevent others from following me and Julie into the abyss unprepared. And those who stubbornly forge ahead need to know they are not alone. A mere mortal woman can't do this alone. We didn't.

3

The Day Christmas
Jumped the Shark for Julie

Kevin was a successful self-made businessman. So was David. They had both overcome financial and other hardships of childhood. In fact, I've come to realize that they're a lot alike. Early on, after hearing so many of Julie's stories about Kevin's daughters, I just figured that what Kevin lacked in parenting skills, he made up for in business. I mean, he was *very* successful when it came to making money. Who could expect him to be the perfect father too? David wasn't as rich, so I was under the delusion he had both sets of skills.

When Julie first started dating Kevin, we talked about their 20-year age difference and how it might matter in the long run. Julie had some experience with that in observing her parents' marriage. Her father was much older than her mother and he was also a successful businessman. I guess it didn't look so bad from her point of view because the only thing that really concerned her was whether or not she wanted children. She wasn't sure, but it wasn't an option with Kevin. He had already had a vasectomy.

I wasn't sure either, but I was leaning toward not having children because I didn't think that I'd have any skills as a mother. I didn't have the best childhood due to the alcoholism of both parents (not always at the same time, but always). They did their best and I'm grateful for that, but they didn't set a great example. Maybe if I had married teen idol Donny Osmond like I planned, he could have shared the kind of family values needed to raise children. But short of marrying Donny, or becoming a Mormon, I knew I didn't have the confidence. I remember sharing that with David. Then I almost fell over when he admitted he never wanted *any* children. So how did he end up with three? *(Note to men readers: Just because you actually have a pair doesn't mean you don't need to GROW A PAIR!!! Gosh, that could be a bumper sticker.)*

I remember when Julie made her decision. It was after a discussion with her mother. Julie admitted she worried about who would take care of her in her old age if she didn't have any children. Her mother pointed out to her that even if you do have children, nothing guarantees they will ever take care of you. Julie's mom could have been Kevin's and David's gypsy fortune teller. Or as they say in Mississippi, "I heard that!"

So Julie and Kevin got married on December 4, 1988. And on that first Christmas as a married couple, she got her first dose of stepmotherhood. The three girls were all in their late teens or early 20s, out of high school either by pregnancy or graduation. Now they wanted a family Christmas at Dad's house. Kevin and Julie said that would be great. But a few days before the 25th, the girls were all upset about it. They told Kevin they felt horrible that their mother would be all alone on Christmas if they were with him and Julie. Their solution was to invite their mother over to Dad's house too.

Now Julie, being a new bride who hadn't quite caught on to the girls' games yet, thought it wouldn't be so bad. Their mother was Kevin's first wife and Julie was the third. Wife number one was 20 years older than Julie and not tall, blonde and pretty like the new Mrs. Winston. I'm sure wife number two could write her own book about Kevin's kids, but she didn't stick around long enough. I sure hope she enjoys reading this one.

Julie planned the perfect dinner, bought the perfect presents, put on her most perfect married smile for the Christmas holiday and played the perfect hostess. Unfortunately, they all took advantage of her perfect hostessing skills and on that day they turned her into the perfect waitress. All afternoon she cooked, filled plates, re-filled glasses and washed dishes. They enjoyed opening the presents Julie had shopped for, without actually thanking or acknowledging her, and reminisced about Christmases past.

And that is the story of when Christmas "jumped the shark" for Julie.

4

What's in a Name?

As our wedding date approached, actually when we went for the license, the talk began.

David asked, "Aren't you going to change your name?"

"I hadn't really thought about it," was what I said. What I meant was, "If you think Kerry Kendall switched from Kerry Kohanowski only to go back to something as unpronounceable as Kerry Hrablicht, you've got to be kidding."

I had changed my last name legally when I was in college and started to search for television jobs because I couldn't get anyone to remember me. And when you want a career in television news, it's really important to stand out. Having a rhythmic name helped. I asked everyone who ever hired me. They said they remembered the name as well as remembering I was a female sportscaster. My first news director said he probably would have hired me as Kerry Kohanowski, but he would have insisted I change my name for his newscast.

I guess it wasn't unusual for a man David's age to expect me to change my name. He's 15 years older than I am. That sad look of his was unfair though. Without saying a word, he made it clear he would be truly hurt if I didn't take on that albatross of a last name.

I had never heard of another name starting with *Hr* except for that of Al Hrabosky, a relief pitcher for the Cardinals, Royals and Braves in the 1970s. They called him the *Mad Hungarian*. He was probably mad about having such a kooky last name. I had a friend whose last name started with *Wd*, but she got rid of that when she got married. And my cousin Dr. Yurchyk, and her husband Dr. Kwiatkowski, changed their last names to Barrett for professional reasons. Really now, wouldn't you be more likely to go to a Dr. Barrett than a Dr. Kwiatkowski or a Dr. Yurchyk? And even after Dr. Yurchyk divorced Dr. Kwiatkowski, now both Drs. Barrett, and married Dr. Nevalainen, (always Nevalainen) she kept the Barrett. Smart move I say. She's now a fairly young, financially secure retiree and I think a lot of her success was the direct result of being a Barrett. After all, it worked for Oliver in *Love Story*.

Back to my dilemma, I think David's "I'll-be-so-hurt" attitude was compounded by his ex-wife taking back her maiden name after the divorce. Eventually, we would find out she took back her name only so she could play the credit card game and default on bills as two people instead of one. Who knows if she used any other names. We've had plenty of creditors calling us, looking for her under her married name, many years after she should not have been using it legally.

Well, I told David I'd think about changing my name. I was trying to buy time to get him to see my point of view. After all, we didn't plan on having children. What was the big deal with me changing my name? Kerry Kendall was so easy and I didn't want to give that up. Besides, google Kerry Kendall on the internet and you'll get some floozy (not me) who once posed for Playboy. I know this because practically the day after the magazine hit the stands, an ex-boyfriend called me to tell me he had seen my centerfold. It's a pretty cool conversation starter.

But if you google for the Kerry Kendall listed on the Internet Movie Data Base, well I don't want anyone mistaking me for that chick. I can only imagine that the parents of that Kerry Kendall are not very proud. She has only one credit as an actress, but it's a memorable one. (You can google her after you finish reading this chapter. I know you will.)

Getting back to the topic at hand again, I guess it was just the old-fashioned custom of taking your husband's name that mattered most to David. Since I was still dabbling in some t.v. work, I told him I'd never change my on-air name. That didn't matter to him. He said he didn't expect me to change my on-air name, just my real name. I was stuck without any more excuses and I felt as if I had to give in. This was my first choose-your-battles-wisely lesson. If he didn't mind that I was Kerry Kendall to the media masses (note the name of the author of this book), I guess I could be Kerry Hrablicht to my husband, the public library, the IRS, the department of motor vehicles and the credit card companies. But my past as both Kerry Kohanowski and Kerry Kendall did nothing to prepared me as Mrs. Hrablicht for what lied ahead.

What's in my past as Kerry Kohanowski? Not much. That is, not much notoriety for anyone with that name. My picture was in the local newspaper several times for school and Girl Scout functions, but you could hardly call that fame. I had the typical student success with awards, the honor roll and dean's list, of course. But I didn't try to kill anyone or rob a bank or do anything that would bring me lasting fame as a Kohanowski.

My father, Wasil Charles Kochanowski, was the only boy born to Paul and Pauline Kochanowski. Grandpa dropped the "c." And you can imagine that my dad, the policeman, only appeared in the police blotter section of the newspaper as the arresting officer. My brother, the only one able to pass on the Kohanowski handle, has always been a stand-up guy. He even has Secret Service clearance for his job as an electrician on the President's helicopter team. His name has only been in the newspaper for awards, or for being on committees during his volunteer firefighting career.

So Kerry Kohanowski had no experience with fame, positive or negative. Kerry Kendall achieved plenty of fame for being one of the few female television sportscasters around in the early '80s. Thankfully, those were only positive experiences, except for that one instance in Syracuse, which is not really worth mentioning. And don't bother googling for it. It was way before the internet captured our every move, thank God.

If only I had held firm. If only I had known then what I know now, I never would have become a *Hrablicht*. A name like that stands out in the police blotter column of the local newspaper in print and online. How many times would it stand out? As of this writing, we're still counting.

5

The Birth of Bucky

I met David's ex-wife at one of Bryan's third grade school music functions about six months into our relationship. It was the first time I was put in the position of meeting an ex and I was a little nervous. At this early stage, I still didn't know much about her. She was the one who initiated the divorce, so I had this vision of a Gloria Steinem type. I expected her to have a modern, confident air about her and be adorned with a few classic Chanel accessories from her housewife days in Fairfield County. At the very least, I thought I'd see a string of pearls and some totally bitchin' shoes. Wrong.

The first Mrs. Hrablicht was tall, thin and quite plain. She looked older than her 40-something years, probably because she had a lot of lip wrinkles from smoking. Her outfit for the evening was all gray. The sweater, skirt, tights and shoes. Gray, gray, gray and gray. She wasn't wearing any jewelry and her shoulder-length hair hung straight. She wore very little make up and overall, she was unremarkable. I was relieved, until I zeroed in on her one remarkable feature: her overbite. *Remarkable* doesn't do it justice. It was *huge*. Wow. None of the kids even had buck teeth. David should have warned me about this. It took all of my self control to keep eye contact instead of looking at her teeth. I kept repeating to myself, "Do not stare at her teeth. Do not stare at her teeth."

When the show was over, we exchanged pleasantries. She brought a date too. But mostly we just listened to Bryan report on things that happened on the stage. This was a very big deal to him and he thought he should be rewarded with an ice cream sundae for his hard work. David and I took him to the local Dairy Queen and his mother left with her date. As I remember, he had very nice teeth. It was a weekend and Bryan was coming home with David to his cousin Emma's house, where David had been living since the divorce.

David and I didn't get any time alone that evening, so I never mentioned *the overbite*. The next night we went out to dinner with David's best friend John and his wife Lexi. John had introduced David and I. He was a childhood friend of David's. John and I became friends when he and Lexi joined the same gym where I worked out. That night at dinner, when Lexi and I went to the ladies' room, I mentioned the overbite. She laughed. She had met David's ex-wife just once when she and John were invited over for dinner. She remembered two things from that night: the overbite and how she didn't serve dinner until 10 p.m. So Lexi wasn't fond of her and we both giggled like schoolgirls about the overbite. Not so much to be mean, but because David didn't warn me and it was so blatantly obvious that he should have.

When we got back to the table, she and I couldn't look at each other without laughing. The guys insisted we let them in on the joke, so I told John about meeting "Bucky."

David knew exactly what I meant and said, "I spent three thousand dollars to fix her teeth."

David's frugality was legendary among the three of us, so I said, "You should have spent five thousand you cheap bastard, because it didn't work."

We all laughed, and from that moment on, Lynn became "Bucky."

After the laughs died down (and believe me, that took awhile), David told us the story of how Lynn got tired of wearing the braces he paid for and had them removed early. He said it was her own fault that her overbite never really got fixed. He also told us that her biggest fear was growing old to look like her mother, who had an impressive overbite of her own. It wasn't until a few months later that I met her mother and understood the fear. Except for her mom's full head of white hair, Lynn looked *exactly* like her. Every time she looked at her mother, she was seeing herself in the future, and that wasn't good. But her mother was very nice to me, so I never resorted to "Bucky Senior" or "Bucky Junior," just "Bucky."

6

Bucky Emails

Hey Julie,

I met David's ex-wife tonight. I'm still reeling from the site of her overbite. I can't believe he didn't tell me about it. I couldn't help staring at her teeth. Yikes. Haven't mentioned it to him yet because Bryan was with us all evening. In fact, I think I'll wait to see if he brings it up.

Kerry

Dear Kerry,

I know EXACTLY what you mean about staring at her teeth. Kevin's first wife keeps losing teeth and she doesn't do anything about it. She must be afraid of the dentist or something. I only see her when I run into her in a store or some other public place, but I swear, she has less and less teeth every time. I've never asked him about it.

Another funny coincidence, huh? Me, you, ex-wives and teeth. I told you to to get out of that relationship. Stop following me. I'm obviously not traveling down the yellow brick road. It's more like a dark path into a very long tunnel.

Julie

Dear Julie,

      Is there a light at the end of that tunnel?

Kerry

Ker,

      Oncoming train. Run.

Julie

7

My First Clue

It should have been my first clue that there were thousands of intrusions to come, but when you have no experience with something, you're clueless. That was me, Clueless Kerry. I felt like I was finally in a great place personally, professionally and emotionally. What could go wrong?

The phone rang at my apartment shortly after David and I decided to get married. It was Bucky, calling to congratulate me. Now an ex calling to congratulate me for being the new Mrs. kind of caught me off guard. I just held on to the phone and listened. What I heard next didn't make sense.

She said, "Cindy has to be in your wedding if you want Bryan to be there."

We hadn't even made any wedding plans yet.

Bryan was 7 years old at the time and spent almost all of his non-school time with his father and me because his mother didn't pay any attention to him. David was retired from banking. It was never a problem for him to have Bryan any day after school until late at night and all throughout the weekend. In fact, the only time his mother insisted on having him was for the holidays.

Bucky would take Jack, Cindy and Bryan to a family gathering at the home of her parents or one of her sisters. She seemed to want to show them that she cared about her kids. At age 7, Bryan didn't know the difference. He was just glad to see his cousins. David and I enjoyed the time alone, but not nearly as much as we enjoyed Bryan's holiday reports. They were hilarious. His stories always ended the same way, with his mother not talking to any of her relatives "ever again." It lasted through the next holiday when she would just stay home with the kids. Then the holiday after that, she'd start talking to her family again and the cycle would continue. One holiday with family, one with just the kids. Of course as the kids got older, the four of them were the ones fighting. But I'll leave those stories for later. Back to the wedding.

Bucky threatened to keep Bryan away from the wedding if Cindy wasn't in it. I hadn't really thought about it, but I did know that at age 37, I wanted a very small wedding and no bridal party. Haven't we all been through the ugly dress thing enough? Although, taking revenge on my old friend Liz, for making me wear a freakin' bustle in her wedding, did cross my mind for a brief moment. However, I ended up asking Rosanne to be my maid of honor because she's one of my dearest friends and I knew it would mean a lot to her. I also told her to wear anything she wanted because I trusted her taste.

What we decided to do with Cindy was to put her on her father's side of the aisle with her brother Jack, the best man, and Bryan, the ring bearer. She could just stand there for all I cared. At this point I really didn't loathe Cindy, but I did resent her mother's meddling.

Cindy was 14 at the time and had already gone through over a year of being her mother's smoking and drinking buddy and partner in crime against her father. I didn't know much about her personally except that she was her mother's puppet. She did everything her mother said and went back and forth between "I need a father in my life" and "I need money" every time she called David on the phone.

Even at this early stage, David recognized her insincerity, though I'm sure it didn't hurt any less. The girl had every opportunity to be close to her father, just like Bryan, but she refused over and over again.

After the divorce, David lived with his cousin Emma and her widowed mother, his Aunt Anna. Aunt Anna, her husband and Emma lived in the same house with David and his parents growing up. So Emma and David were as close as brother and sister and she was glad to have him back. David admits that he neglected his own family during his first marriage because they were always with Bucky's family.

Emma has a very welcoming nature and her home was always open to the kids and to me. She invited Cindy over many times, as did David. Cindy always said she'd come, but she never did, except at Christmas. That might have had something to do with the presents Emma bought. Her shopping skill is a Christmas miracle. She always picks out perfectly thoughtful and useful gifts and Cindy always came to collect. But unless it was Christmas, we didn't see Cindy. David saw her every time he picked up Bryan and brought him back to his mother's place. He also took her out to dinner once in awhile, but not often. She accepted his dinner invitations, but she usually backed out at the last minute with some ridiculous excuse.

At the time of the wedding, Cindy's drunken episodes had not yet begun. It was the violent tantrums that started first, a few months before the wedding. Those tantrums triggered a series of panic attacks in David that have lessened in intensity, but have never ended.

8

Panic Attacks

These days the panic attacks take the form of headaches, migraines, stomach aches, dizzy spells, possible gout attacks, aches and pains of varying degrees, sleeping sickness, everything but depression.

"I'm not depressed. I'm just tired," he says.

Tired my ass. Tired is sleeping 10 hours after a long, restless night. Depressed is sleeping more than 13 hours every day after either a peaceful night or a fitful night.

The panic attacks began in the summer of 1997 when I gave David the ultimatum about getting married or moving on. (Just a coincidence. Really.) He wanted to "live together." Yeah right, just as soon as we're married. Looking back, that saved him. I would have left him that first year if we weren't married. In fact, I seriously thought about leaving him anyway and cutting my losses. It would have been hard for me to fail at something as big as marriage. Not wanting to go through that kept me with him and I thank God for that. He needed me, and I think I needed to go through those very tough early days to realize just how much I love him.

The first panic episode came one night after he drove Bryan home after a Wednesday night visit. For some still unknown reason, Cindy got terribly violent when David brought Bryan in. David said she kept yelling at him, blaming him for everything. What everything? Who knows? She was just enraged and kept hitting him and he couldn't calm her down so he just left. He said her mother chimed in too, but with nothing specific. When he got home, he was very upset. Perhaps it was a combination of emotions and blood pressure, but whatever it was, he started to feel sick. I told him to lie down and he got through the night with nothing more than a little restlessness. This was probably the first panic attack nipped in the bud. The next one ended in the hospital just days later.

We were out driving in Redding, Connecticut near the home we were about to move into after the wedding. David built it as an investment, but it wasn't sold, so it was ours for now. Redding is a very rural area that's hard to get around, if you're used to typical city blocks. We went out to meet one of the contractors to lead him to the house. We had David's car, a Honda Civic 4-speed stick shift that I couldn't drive without stripping the gears.

We met the contractor a few miles from home and got out of the car to say hello. Before we got back into the car, David grabbed his chest and said he felt like he was having a heart attack. This was before either of us carried a cell phone. The contractor knocked on the closest door and, thankfully, a fireman with medical training lived there and calmed David down while we waited for the ambulance to arrive. David had me convinced this was really a heart attack and I started to feel guilty about not getting him some medical attention the previous Wednesday night. The ambulance took him to Danbury Hospital and the contractor drove me home in David's car so I could get mine, drive him back to his truck, and continue on to the hospital. I never did learn to drive a stick shift.

At the hospital, they determined that although he did not have a heart attack, something was wrong. They admitted him for a whole battery of tests and the doctors said it would be a good idea not to have any visitors who would upset him. So the kids and ex were off limits, yet David said he had to talk to the boys just in case his days were numbered. After he made that call, everyone knew he was in the hospital and they kept calling to find out what was wrong. You'd think Cindy would at least apologize for her behavior the previous week. Nope. She just continued her badgering over the phone and David had to stop answering. I tried to tell Bucky that he needed rest and respite from Cindy. She seemed to understand, but nothing is as it seems with people like her and Cindy and later, Bryan.

Ultimately David was released with the understanding that this was a panic attack brought on by stress and he needed to get control of his life or start on some kind of anti-anxiety medication. David, being a typical man, figured he could control this.

The second panic attack happened while I was at work, teaching school in Newtown. David was at his cousin Emma's house in Milford, about 25 miles away. They tracked me down at work and when I got on the phone, David sounded like he was dying. Well, he didn't *sound* so bad, he was *talking* like he was dying. He asked me to leave work and come over right away. When I got there, Emma and his oldest son, Jack, were at his bedside and David was attempting to go over his finances with them because he was convinced he was going to have a heart attack and die at any moment. So I took him to the hospital.

In the emergency room they did an EKG and kept a monitor on him for his vitals and found he was having another panic attack. He wasn't convinced. He was still at death's door, according to him, Dr. David.

Now let me digress for a moment. On the up side, the panic attacks have made David more attentive to his physical health. He lets me know about every ache and pain, unlike most men who wait until their wives force them to see a doctor. And he'll research drugs and ailments on the internet regularly.

Almost 20 years later, chest pains from a hiatal hernia made David seek out a consultation with a cardiologist as well as his internist.

The cardiologist prescribed the standard low dose of aspirin for a 60-year-old man. The internist ran a whole slew of tests and found out he needed thyroid meds as well as a continuation of his blood pressure and anti-anxiety meds. My penny-pinching husband has a thing about saving money everywhere, even on medicine. Now I don't mean just getting generics, I mean low-dosing. Whatever is prescribed for him, he takes half of the dose. He's a champion pill splitter.

On our follow-up appointment with the cardiologist, the doctor asked him for a list of his current meds, vitamins and any supplements. David had a long hand-written list ready for him, but the doctor noticed that the dosages were not right for someone of David's age and weight. And then David bragged about only needing half a pill of this or half a pill of that. The cardiologist looked at him as if to say, "and what medical degree do you have that gives you the knowledge to determine the dosage?" But before he could even ask, I said, "Doctor, you don't understand the situation here. You are merely a *consultant* to Dr. David. He knows what's best. Just ask him." The doctor laughed and shook his head. That was our last visit with the cardiac *consultant*.

Okay, the panic attack adventure continues. After these panic attacks, it was as if David was super sensitive to every ache and pain, whether real or imagined, and most of them were imagined. Although I wasn't over it yet either. I mean, the doctors could be wrong. It's happened before. What if he was having heart problems that couldn't be diagnosed *because* of his panic attacks? I kept telling myself that I couldn't let something like that kill him. It would be my fault. So I was still along for the ride.

The next ride came a few months later. Once again it was after emotional turmoil with the co-dependent daughter and ex-wife. They were, and still are, quite a pair. This was a big one. Ever since the divorce, which Bucky initiated, she had made Cindy her confidant and smoking and drinking buddy. I guess she didn't see any problem in sharing her cigs and wine with a young teenager whom she took into her confidence enough to plan out the child molestation accusation.

Oh yeah. David had told me that she pulled this in the lawyer's office when they were going through the final points of the divorce. She accused him of molesting Cindy but said she was willing to forget it if he gave her more money. He walked out and she never filed charges, but the accusation alone broke his heart. From then on, and I mean 20-plus years of "then on," every time either one of the women was drinking, they'd call and mention it. After they sobered up, Cindy would be the one to call and apologize and admit that her mother put her up to it just to try and get more money from Dad.

It was after one of these drunken phone calls from Cindy that David went into another downward spiral. Her calls were always late at night, so sleep for me was out of the question. I had to talk him out of his symptoms or drive him to the hospital. At this point, a hospital visit was more efficient because he still wasn't able to accept the fact that the only thing wrong with him was in his head. So off we went. The outcome was the same for him, but this time I got better. I stopped thinking that there would ever be a heart attack because the panic attacks were likely to kill him first.

The last hospital visit for a panic attack came the following winter when David, Bryan and I were at a basketball game at my high school. We weren't dealing with any immediate turmoil, but David did have to see Bucky and Cindy when he picked Bryan up that afternoon and he knew he'd be seeing them again when he took Bryan home. In his often-agitated state, that was sometimes enough to set him off. The *girls* were acting more like drinking buddies than mother and daughter.

The janitor had just washed the floor in the stairway leading to my classroom. On our trip down to show Bryan around, David slipped and fell. Not a big deal, but before we left to go home, he was complaining of chest pains again and his panic attack triggered a cold sweat. So I drove him to the hospital. But this time I parked just outside the emergency entrance, left Bryan in the car, brought David in and told the nurse, "Call me when he's finished." I took Bryan home with me. I was done allowing the panic attacks to happen.

That was our last trip to the hospital. Lesson learned. Unfortunately, not by David. It would be years before he could choose to ignore the madness that would cause such symptoms.

9

"Goot for You!"

My former psychiatrist, Dr. Tarique Perera, definitely saved my marriage. Of course there are days that I'd like to string him up and beat him for that. But overall, it's worked out. Because I've stayed married to David, I've been able to delve into layers of humor in the human psyche that other people can only dream of, or read about. I can find humor in everything, even watching my husband get arrested. Years later, I still laugh out loud at the memory. And the phrase, "Good for you!" said with a slight Indian accent, sends me into hysterics

We were invited to a wedding at a restaurant in Newtown, the town in which I taught television production. Yes, just about every week my name would scroll across the t.v. screens of Newtown after some high school production. They might not have been able to pronounce it, but it certainly was recognizable. A big *Hr* followed by some other letters

It was the wedding of one of David's co-workers and the cocktail hour began at 6 p.m. David had taken a job in the mortgage business shortly after we got married. Bryan had some kind of school sports function, so David couldn't be there on time because I refused to drive the kid. It was dad's turn, for once. Thanks to Dr. Perera, I stopped running my life around either of their schedules and decided to take my own car to the cocktail hour and let David join me later. The cocktails weren't the draw. Neither one of us is a big drinker. It's just that his co-workers were fun folks and I wouldn't feel out of place without him. David came about an hour later and we had a nice time together too. Good people, good food, good music and like always, we had had enough by about 11 p.m. We're not big party people. I think we only had about two drinks each and we both ate a full meal, so driving impaired was not an issue. But it was a cold, dark, winter night and I asked him if he wanted to take one car home and come back tomorrow for the other. He said, "No, just follow me."

One of the side effects of David's suppressed anger at his children is his road rage. Even now, many years after his symptoms of divorced-parent-guilt reared their ugly head, no one will get into a car or golf cart when he's driving except me. And that's only because I get more material for my book. One day when he neglected to stop at a stop sign in our lovely golf cart community, an elderly man in another cart *politely* pointed that out to him. My husband yelled at the old guy, "Bite me!" Nice, huh. Now back to the wedding reception in Newtown, which we had left around 11 p.m.

There was some kind of roadblock at the bottom of the hill close to the restaurant. I was about five cars behind David, on top of the hill, which turned out to be the best vantage point for all the action. Several other cars in front of David followed the policeman's instructions and turned left. David wanted to go straight. I rolled down the window in the freezing cold, still night and strained my ears to hear what was going on. David was yelling at the police officer, asking *why* he had to turn left. Why? What the heck does it matter? Just turn left, you idiot! But no, not my idiot. So the officer gets him out of the car, pushes him down on the trunk and puts handcuffs on him. I felt like I was watching the opening of some television cop show and they forgot to play the theme song. The *Candid Camera* show had done some stunts in Newtown before. My friend Joyce got caught in a pretty good one. But Peter Funt and his camera crew were nowhere to be seen on this night. I wondered what I should do.

I had to decide quickly. Get out, run down the hill and interfere, hopefully sparing my husband some pain and suffering? Nah. He already had the cuffs on. What could I do? Scream and cry like an hysterical wife? Of course not. Thanks to Dr. Perera, I was medicated and prepared for events such as this. So what would the good doctor tell me to do? He would tell me not to interfere and to let David suffer the consequences of his own behavior. Of this, I was certain. So that's what I did. I drove by as David was put into the back of a patrol car and I turned left. No questions asked. I went around the block and went back to the wedding.

I found David's boss, Sean, a young man with connections to everyone everywhere, and told him the story. Aware of David's poor mental health and short temper due to his mutant offspring, Sean had a good laugh. Then he told me he had a friend on the Newtown police force, a sergeant, and everything would be taken care of. He'd make a phone call and I should go home and wait to hear from him. So I did.

Just after midnight, Sean called, slightly amused I think, to tell me there was nothing he could do. He said his friend the cop told him that David was behaving like such an asshole that there was no way they were going to let him off. Great. Now what? I thanked Sean and told him I'd fill him in later.

So what would Dr. Perera tell me to do now? I know. He'd say, "Get a good night's sleep." I was probably going to need it. So I went to bed.

At about 3 a.m. David called and said, "Can you pick me up?"

"Where are you?" I asked, feigning ignorance.

"The Newtown police station," he said. He sounded awful.

When I arrived, he was ready to go and didn't speak. He looked like he had been crying. We got into the car and I pulled out of the parking lot in silence. After a few minutes, he told me everything was going to be alright. He said it was a misunderstanding and both he and the officer got a little heated in an exchange at a roadblock and they ended up apologizing to each other. I didn't ask too much and he explained that all he did was to ask what the road block was about, and the officer got mad that he asked. I think the officer got mad that he asked repeatedly and loudly and caused a traffic jam. But hey, that's just me.

There are more details to this story, but they're not important. Let's just sum it up by saying the ol' highly recognizable *Hr* name got into the police blotter section of the local Newtown paper, the very local weekly which everyone in Newtown reads from cover to cover in the town in which I teach, where my name scrolls across the television screens weekly.

David's lawyer, a wonderful real estate lawyer, who appears to be clueless in the areas of criminal law and divorce, advised him *not* to take a breathalyzer test. When you refuse to take the test in Connecticut, you're automatically charged with a DUI. Yep, my husband got arrested for driving under the influence, even though I'm sure he wasn't. That is, I'm sure he wasn't under the influence of alcohol, just under the influence of the second generation *Hr* delinquents who were sucking the life out of him and had drained his patience and altered his temperament. He had panic attacks, anxiety attacks, and he lashed out at anyone for the smallest thing. He directed his anger at everyone except the source: his three children.

Days later in Dr. Perera's office, I told him the whole story about David's arrest. Dr. Perera is a good listener. He doesn't interject much and he laughs in just the right places, which made my therapy sessions quite enjoyable for both of us. When I got to the part about my husband getting handcuffed, Dr. Perera was on the edge of his seat and couldn't help interrupting.

"What did you do?" he asked.

I told him I drove right by and went around the block and back to the wedding. He could hardly contain his amusement. If it weren't for his professionalism, I truly believe he would have hit the floor on his knees and rolled around in hysterics.

"Goot for you!" he said. I took that to be, "Good for you," with his Indian accent.

Finally, a breakthrough for me, thanks to therapy, medication and my newly found ability to set boundaries. I would not be dragged down and into the web of enabling either stepchildren or my husband. I was taking care of me and *goot for me!*

But that's not the best part. The best part is that I was able to express this feeling to everyone. My psychiatrist had said, "Goot for you!" I was going to enjoy the affirmation.

About a month later, I told this story to very dear friends over dinner one night. I was so pleased with my own breakthrough at the end. That was my punch line, "Good for you!" What I honestly didn't realize was that David had never heard this story. He just lived it. He didn't know I witnessed the whole event. He didn't know that *I knew* he was being held at the police station for most of the night. He didn't know that Sean, for once, could not pull any strings to help him out. He didn't know it until this very night at dinner. And I was so caught up in the progress I had made in my therapy that I didn't even think about that. I guess I should have. Boy was he mad! He erupted with anger.

"You mean you watched them take me away and you didn't do anything?" he yelled across the table.

"Really honey, what could I do? I was five cars back and I really couldn't tell what was going on," I said innocently.

"You didn't do anything? You didn't come and get me?" He couldn't believe it.

It took me forever to explain to him that he missed the point of the whole story. Actually, the point of the whole episode in my opinion, including how I was able to tell the story at this dinner party.

It was *not* about *him*. This was an event in *my* life. It was about me and my breakthrough that I had achieved after months of therapy. I no longer felt the need to rescue him from a situation of his own making. You dug your own hole buster. Crawl out of it. I drove by and saved myself, *my* sanity, *my* pride, *my* composure.

"You should be grateful," I said to him. "I saved your wife."

Honest to God that man did not speak to me for a week. But every blessed moment of David's silent treatment was a gift. It gave me the quiet time and solitude to truly appreciate how far I had come.

On the inside, I kept hearing those three beautiful words repeating loud and clear as if they were coming out of a bullhorn, "Goot for you!" Yep, finally, good for me!

10

Teamwork

There's a line from the movie *The Graduate* where Dustin Hoffman's character, Benjamin, asks Elaine, played by Katherine Ross, how her fiancé proposed to her.

She says, "He said he thought we'd make a pretty good team."

Benjamin laughs and says, "Oh no. He said that?"

His tone implies that it was a stupid proposal. I disagree. In fact, I've disagreed every time I've watched that movie. I always thought it was a perfect proposal for someone who's looking for a partner for the rest of his life. The first time David and I watched the movie together, I pointed that out to him. I was pleased that he agreed. It takes a team effort to have a long and happy marriage and there are plenty of you-and-me-against-the-world issues to deal with. A teammate is not a bad thing to have.

I don't think there can be true equality in any marriage. Team members have varying degrees of talent, strengths and weaknesses. Put 'em all together when the planets are aligned right and you've got a winner like the New York Yankees. But if someone is not pulling his weight or looking to jump ship, or if the whole organization has no support, you've got the dreaded Chicago Cubs, perennial losers. David was a banker. It was a no-brainer to let him handle the finances while I did the cooking, cleaning, shopping and home repairs. He also did the outdoor work like shoveling snow, mowing the grass, chopping wood, most of the dog walking and the bug killing. We both scooped the litter boxes. Oh, there was that one time when he ran like a little girl and left me to deal with a few bats in our bedroom. But except for that, we're usually a pretty good team.

Considering David and I didn't meet until I was 34, he knew that I was capable of surviving the financial world without him. I wasn't playing the stock market or anything like that. I was working a full-time teaching job and occasionally some part-time broadcasting jobs. I had a retirement account, deposited my paychecks in the bank, used credit cards, paid my bills on time and *had no debt*. I know he valued that. He actually said so. What I didn't realize was that it *totally amazed him*. A woman who could handle the flow of money without going into debt was a blessed novelty to him. When we got married, we merged. He had a whole lot more than I did, but I think we merged easily because he knew I was responsible on my own.

Over the years David has asked for my opinion on the financial moves he wants to make with our investments. I tell him what I think, but I also tell him that I will defer to him because he's more educated on those matters. Occasionally, he takes the time to school me on our current financial situation. I listen. Sometimes I take notes. But I never worry. We're both conservative and pretty much on the same page when it comes to investing.

Once, in our 14th year of marriage, he insisted I learn all the details of our financial situation. So I got a notebook and wrote down everything he said about every account. It was tiring, and I didn't fully comprehend the details, but I did write them down in plain English so I could handle anything (with the help of our professional financial adviser) if David wasn't around.

After we finished, he said, "The last time I did this, I got served divorce papers right after. She was smart enough to wait and see where all the money was."

"She wasn't that smart," I said. "I'd never give up half of all this. I'd slowly poison you, wait for you to die, and then I'd get it all."

He laughed. Yay team!

11

Let's Do Lunch

Bucky's divorce from David was premeditated. That's the only pro-active thing I've ever known her to do. She was squirreling away money in the months before it happened and, thanks to David's tutoring, she was fully aware of their finances in order to prepare her lawyer for the end. David, on the other hand, still trusted his wife with that financial schooling he gave her, and the only lawyer he ever used specialized in real estate. He was about to get royally screwed, but it was his own fault.

Let me take a moment here to talk to the men who might be reading this. Or if you're a woman who has a brother or a male friend you care about, clue him in.

Gentlemen, if you choose to marry a woman who only has a high school education and no ambition to work, or to learn how to support herself in this world, you'll get what you deserve. And believe me, it's going to cost you. And it should.

As my favorite financial minister Dave Ramsey says, "You've got to pay a stupid tax." If you want to take care of something helpless, damn it, get a kitten. The days of helpless women are over. Even the ones who are unable to take care of themselves are perfectly capable of using *your* money to hire a female, Jewish lawyer to look out for their interests in a divorce. You and your real estate lawyer will be left with *bupkes*.

Now let's review Bucky's capacity to take care of herself after the divorce.

She ended up with a check for over $650,000, the contents of the house, a car, and child support for three children. So she started spending. She bought a much-too-expensive house in a beach community in Fairfield County, the most expensive county in Connecticut and one of the most expensive in the nation. She also took out a mortgage. Eventually, she realized she couldn't afford the house or the mortgage because she had no income and no skills with which to get an income. So she moved. Not to a smaller less expensive house in a more moderately priced section of town. She moved to another house on the next block. Almost as expensive. She said she didn't want the kids to leave their neighborhood. Soon after, she moved again. Yep, you guessed it, third house, same neighborhood, but a little more inland. Without an actual view of the beach, this one must have been a bargain. Three moves in less than three years.

Even Bryan, at ages 5, 6 and 7, thought it was strange. On his weekend and after-school visits with his dad, we'd often hear him say, "Mom's moving again and no one wants to help her." Then he'd tell us how all of her relatives swore they'd never lift another piece of furniture for her again. Ah, but there were many more moves to come. And Bryan was right. The number of movers has gone down significantly over the years.

Eventually, she couldn't afford the third house and the bank was after her for the payments. So she turned to the source she always used for money, the Bank of David.

The day Bucky called to invite David to lunch, I figured it was to talk about the kids. Well, it was, sort of. We weren't married yet, so it was during the first three years of our relationship and at this point I still didn't know how a woman like this operated. From what

I had heard, she seemed to have no pride, no integrity, no honor, no responsibility for herself or her children and their behavior. This was foreign to me and I wasn't ready to accept it. I often thought that I had to be missing something. I didn't know anyone like her.

David came over to my place after the big lunch and he was just giddy with laughter. Yes, giddy is the only way to describe him.

I said, "What did she do, stick you with the check?"

"No," he said, "She paid for her own lunch but she wants me to buy her a house."

"A what?" I said.

"A house," he repeated, laughing out loud. "I told her I'd have to discuss it with you."

Well, this definitely topped the time she asked him to pay to send her to school. It was soon after the divorce and I suppose she had one moment of clarity when she realized she had no marketable skills. Finally she wanted an education. David said she had no interest in learning anything before the divorce, so he told her to pay for her own education with her settlement and the money she skimmed off their accounts before she even got her settlement. But back to the request for the house.

He said, at first he thought it was a joke, and he really laughed out loud. Then she started to explain the very good reasons she thought she deserved a house purchased by the man she stole plenty of money from already. A man who tried to give her advice on living within her means with over half a million dollars so she wouldn't be in this situation. I wish I could have heard her well-rehearsed soliloquy.

It seems she had a plan that David would buy her a house and let her and the kids live in it until the youngest, Bryan, turned 18 and then David could sell it. When he told me this, I just lost it. Hysterical with laughter, for once I had no comeback and believe me, it's hard to render me speechless. I just couldn't imagine anyone having the chutzpah to ask her ex-husband to buy her a house.

I've got to admit, it's a helluva plan. But the shear gall of her request sent us on a little mission of our own: Follow the money. Where was it going? It was less than three years since the divorce. Didn't she still have some of that $650,000 and a continuous flow of child support and alimony? By our own observations and our gentle prodding of the children we tried to figure it out.

Bucky didn't have nice clothes and neither did the kids. Even though David insisted she always shopped at the expensive department stores, I couldn't tell. I used to see her at Bryan's school events and believe me, she didn't dress to impress. She also wasn't spending it on her hair or nails. I'm sure she bought Cindy whatever she wanted for her wardrobe. According to David, Cindy always got everything she wanted from her mother regardless of the cost. David said she never catered to either of the boys like she did to Cindy. Jack also recognized that early on. Jack was getting more and more independent and he probably spent his pizza delivery money on himself instead of asking his mother for anything. David bought most of Bryan's clothes except for what he got from his mother, or David's cousin Emma, for his birthday and Christmas.

There was a little spending spree right after she got her divorce settlement check. Jack got a new car which probably set her back $15,000. That was her first attempt to buy his loyalty against his father. But I'm sure she didn't pay cash for it. And really, $650,000 minus $15,000? Well, you get the point. She was probably planning to stick the kid with the payments, but that didn't happen. Give a teenage, pothead pizza deliverer a brand new car for no reason and you'd better make sure he has a sense of responsibility and the intellect to value that car. After all, it was the means by which to deliver those pizzas. Unfortunately, car and driver did not have a very long relationship. Funny how drag racing under the influence can turn a brand new car into a worthless hunk of twisted metal.

Bucky herself had car payments on a Volvo, not a Ferrari. And in the fourth year since the divorce, which was our first year of marriage, there was a Ford when the Volvo disappeared. I don't know what happened to the Volvo, but I know the Ford was not paid for. The loan company kept mistakenly calling our number regarding the late payments. We also got some calls about credit card bills for awhile. And when we told her about the calls, they stopped. Logically, you'd assume she started paying those bills, right? Wrong. She went back to using her maiden name so no one made the mistake of calling us anymore. And that gave her the added bonus of spending twice as much, since she wasn't paying for anything anyway.

The kids always went to public school and she wasn't paying for anything extra like ballet, karate or sports. The extra stuff was bought and paid for by David.

She didn't seem to spend it on vacations. After one trip to Disney World when she first got her big check, the only place she took the kids was to Rhode Island. Once in a while she'd drive them to some beach town and stay in what Bryan called "a crummy motel." He also offered up the observation that mom and Cindy went through an awful lot of wine and cigarettes on vacation.

So after David and I discussed it (like he promised), we decided her fiscal irresponsibility precluded her from receiving even one more house from David. You may not be surprised by our decision, but she was. And we never really tracked down all that money except to assume it was treated as disposable income when some of it should have been invested for her own future.

After the third house was history, Bucky, Cindy and Bryan moved on to a series of apartments. Jack left and moved in with a roommate in the same town. He had to stay within driving distance of the pizza parlor and all his customers.

The apartments were still in the town of Fairfield, but they got closer and closer to the industrial side of town near Bridgeport which is a world away from Fairfield in status. This was a real step down for a woman who had lived with her family in Westport, Ridgefield and the wealthy side of Fairfield. Too bad she didn't use her suburban housewife days wisely. All three towns have perfectly good libraries and adult education programs. If she took advantage of them, she might have gotten a clue as to how to survive for more than three years on over half a million dollars without losing your home.

The requests for more money continued unanswered for the most part, except for one rainy night during the start of baseball season when Bryan was in the fifth grade. Bucky had called several times during the day and, thanks to caller ID, we didn't answer.

It must have been after 7 p.m. when we settled in to watch the Yankees game and there was a knock at the door. Rarely does anything interrupt my husband during his Yankee games, so I answered the door. It was pouring rain and Bucky was standing there without an umbrella asking to see David. I told her to come in. She said she'd rather wait outside. I told her that was ridiculous and pointed out the weather, just in case she missed it. (Insert your own jokes here about not having the sense to come in from the rain.) She repeated that she'd wait outside. David took his time. I think there were men on base with less than two outs. He eventually went outside, with an umbrella for himself, to see what she wanted. She told him that Bryan had a field trip the next day and she had absolutely no spending money to give him.

He took out his wallet and gave her $20. And if there really was a field trip, I'm betting that she gave Bryan $5.

12

Emails about Gadgets and Money

Dear Julie,

Well David almost blew a gasket when he saw the phone bill yesterday. That caller ID box we've been enjoying is costing us $8.25 a month. He thought it was just part of the regular phone service. "That's $99 a year!" He said he can't believe we were spending that amount of money just to see who was calling us. I reminded him that it's because of Bucky and the 3 Stooges that I got the service and pointed out that he *always* looks at it before picking up the phone too. He said he didn't care who called. "It's stupid." He told me to call the phone company and cancel it tomorrow.

Kerry

P.S. I didn't actually refer to his kids as the 3 Stooges. I said "children." Besides, they're actually just 2 Stooges and Bryan (so far).

Hey Ker,

Hate to side with David on this one but maybe you should stop spending so much of *his* hard-earned money on those new-fangled gadgets just to make *your* life easier.

Hey, did David get you get a new butter churn for your birthday? I hope it's the same color as your washboard. It looks so much nicer when everything in your kitchen matches. I mean, we spend so much time there and all.

Julie

Jules,

I'm keeping the caller ID. (Like there was ever a doubt!)

David just asked me to set the alarm for him for 9:30 tomorrow morning. That's the time he wants to get up and get ready to play golf. I always set the alarm for him before I leave for work. And I've been doing it for free. Not anymore. He's getting a bill slipped under the clock tomorrow: Kerry's Wake Up Service, $8.50/month. I might as well make a little profit to cover my pain and suffering.

And yes, both the churn and washboard are red.

Kerry

13

Damn that Carol Brady

C arol Brady is an evil television character who lied to all of us. She made stepmotherhood look fun and easy. I think re-runs of the *Brady Bunch* should run with a disclaimer that says:

> The story you are about to see is not true. The truth is: *Dad Mike* was gay and died of AIDS. *Mom Carol* once went on a date with the guy who played her stepson, *Greg*. *Marcia* became a drug addict and has admitted to exchanging sex for cocaine (*Marcia, Marcia, Marcia!*). *Peter* keeps coming back to television in the most god-awful reality shows, and he's currently divorcing his third wife. *Cindy* has gone through two husbands. For reasons known only to her, *Jan* has chosen not to show up for several Brady reunions. It appears *Bobby* turned out okay, probably due to his Mormon family values.

> The *Brady Bunch* "happy family" couldn't be further from the truth. In fact, the family dog was even written out of the show for being too difficult to work with.

Not too long ago, Julie and I heard about the downfall of Angie, the second wife of our old friend Jim, and the stepmother to

Jim's three distinguished dependents. We wish we got to her in time. We'd like to think we could have saved her.

Jim is another Mississippi television veteran. That's where Julie and I met him, in Jackson. He and Kelly divorced many years ago and then Jim married Angie, who is 16 years younger than he is. Julie and I lost touch with Jim for awhile. That's why we didn't get to poor Angie in time. Jim says when someone used to ask Angie about getting into the "blended" family situation, she'd scream, "Run!" Too bad she didn't take her own advice. After a five-year marriage, she traded in Jim for two younger models and has started to blaze a trail of shoplifting arrests and DUIs. Before her time with Jim and his three kids, she was a career woman who didn't have so much as a parking ticket on her record. Stepmotherhood clearly pushed her over the edge.

Jim turned out to be a successful salesman after his dalliance in television. In other words, he has money. Or he had money until he started spending it on the children his ex-wife raised in an environment filled with alcohol and drugs.

Let me take a minute here to try and convince you of the superior strength of a mother's bond to children who never grow up. No matter what I've seen Bucky do to her kids, they only turn on her when they need a break from her. During this break, they are often rational and honest about how their mother has tainted their lives. Yet, they always go back to her. It's got to be a freak of nature. If they didn't go back to someone whom they found unworthy before, they probably would go forward. I've looked for a parallel in the animal community, but I can't find one. Dogs and cats don't go back, they move forward and make new friends and have new families with great stepparents. If pack animals cut one out of the herd, the exiled one moves on and starts its own herd or dies. So why do children raised by a mother who uses them, not see the light and leave her in the dust?

Getting back to Jim's brood, he has two girls and a boy. Joe is the oldest and he flunked out of college, but not before cheating his father and his fraternity brothers out of a whole bunch of money that supposedly was needed for school. When Jim finally closed his wallet, Joe stopped speaking to him. It's been over three years and Jim hasn't heard from him. Joe is 27.

Rebecca is now 24 and finally got her GED after dropping out of high school. Jim says, "She could teach classes on how to rip off your father for car repairs." Jim finally caught on and now Rebecca doesn't have a car, but that's okay with her.

She says, "I'm comfortable where I am in my life. I don't need a car." That *comfort* comes from continuing to live with her mother. Rebecca started going to cosmetology school, but has a problem with attendance. She no longer speaks to her dad either, for the same reason as her brother Joe. The money stopped. But she works from time to time, cutting hair without a license.

Beth is the third child, and when she was 17, Jim actually went to court to fight her mother for custody. She testified about her mom's drug use and alcoholism. Her mom's attorney also made Beth testify, in open court, about her own sexual activity. It was a traumatic experience and $77,000 worth of legal expenses later for Jim, Beth went back to her mom. As of this writing, Beth is 21 and she's in her second session of in-patient detox for heroin. She doesn't speak to Jim either. Something about not getting any money from him.

Jim is relishing the quiet in his life for the moment. He knows it won't last. But he says being shut out by all three children, just because he stopped financing their bad behavior, has brought him peace. He's practically serene. He's also says he's the happiest he's ever been in a relationship. The new woman is Jeannie. Julie and I will be taking her out to lunch soon, and maybe shopping, at a book store.

The role of a stepmother is not easy, despite the glorified media versions. It's especially difficult when the biological mother tries her best to undermine your good intentions. She does this for her own amusement, I guess. She doesn't understand that you actually want her kids to succeed and get on with their lives and out of yours. She's willing to use them against you and their father, and nothing short of an exorcism will get them away from her. The kind of manipulation the kids learn by watching her must look attractive, because they all try it out as a career. Some of them make it their life's work.

I actually haven't had much contact with Bucky over the years. I decided long ago that she's not worth my time. I let David handle her. He was pretty good at just avoiding her or ignoring her. We didn't do anything as a family with her, mostly because one or more of the kids always had an "issue" at the time of graduations or other celebrations. The kids generally stayed under their mom's spell and David and I attended special events together, as visitors.

My friend Leslie, the one mentioned in the prologue of this book, who also didn't get out in time, wasn't as lucky. Things like birthdays and graduations were celebrated as a family and Leslie was expected to attend as Dad's new wife. Leslie is a highly intelligent, well-educated, management professional. But as a stepmother, just like me and Julie, she had no clue that she had a target on her back.

Every gathering included remarks from Ron's ex-wife about how the three boys might have to live with their father soon. When they got married, Ron moved into Leslie's small two-bedroom home with her and her teenage daughter. So the threat of taking in three more kids caused some tension. The ex also ranted about how unfair it was that Leslie's daughter got to go to college, even though it was Leslie's college-fund savings and scholarships that made that possible, and Ron's boys never showed any interest in college.

Leslie put up with a lot of shit when it came to money, like we all do. Ron's divorced-father guilt made him pay child support several years beyond what he should have for each of his boys. Leslie was okay with that. It wasn't much because Ron wasn't making much at the time of the divorce. But after the boys graduated from high school, they somehow got the idea that they didn't have to do anything *except* ask dad for money.

The middle child twice convinced Ron that he wanted to go on to higher education. So Ron paid for a semester of community college.

The kid flunked out. Then he decided what he really wanted to study was massage therapy. So Ron paid for a semester at a private massage therapy school too. The kid flunked out again.

Julie and I were so impressed that we allowed Leslie to win the crown that time. After all, it takes a special kid to fail back rubs. It was Leslie's one and only victory because Ron stopped the flow of money. And guess what happened? All three of the boys got full-time jobs with health benefits. They also got girlfriends and apartments and their own lives. And on Father's Day, they take Ron *and Leslie* out for dinner and pick up the check.

Kind of makes you wonder what would happen if Kevin and David stopped the flow of money, doesn't it? It's the dream I live for.

14

Daddy Welfare, Faith and Fate

The experience of being in the same world with David's and Kevin's offspring has led me to widen my scope of education. I have looked up tons of things I'm not actually interested in, just because they touch my life. Things like recreational drugs, narcissistic personality disorder, co-dependency, suicide, welfare, etc. Here's what I found when I searched the history of welfare in the United States. It provides a parallel for what I observed in my own home.

http://www.welfareinfo.org/history/

Throughout the 1800's welfare history continued when there were attempts to reform how the government dealt with the poor. Some changes tried to help the poor move to work rather than continuing to need assistance. Social casework, consisting of caseworkers visiting the poor and training them in morals and a work ethic, was advocated by reformers in the 1880s and 1890s.

Yikes! There it is in the last sentence of that paragraph. "Training them in morals and a work ethic." That's what David's and Kevin's children did not get. The puzzling question is, why not? People knew about this in the 1880's. How could two smart guys like Kevin and David be so oblivious to the basic concept and not try to pass this on to their children? The answer is that, in their worlds, daddy's money trumps all. Daddy's money is the answer, regardless of the question. The kids learned that very well. In fact, it's the only thing they learned well. And they can't get beyond that to learn anything for themselves until the flow of daddy's money stops. Ay, there's the rub. The flow of daddy's money has never stopped so they're stuck in limbo without training in morals and a work ethic. They have no reason to help themselves, so they don't.

I'm not surprised that David's kids ask their father for money. I don't want to say that a bank is all he's ever been to them, but from what I've observed, it's tragically true.

When they're little, kids imitate their parents. Getting money from David was something their mother did all the time. I doubt very much that she hid it from them. Heck, she probably bragged about it in front of them.

I know I asked my parents for money when I was a kid. But I didn't always get it because my mom and dad didn't always have it to give. Dad worked full-time and he also had a part-time job as my brother and I were growing up. Neither of the jobs paid a lot. Mom worked part-time around our school schedule. I learned early on that the best way to get money was to work for it. Looking back, it was actually one of the easiest lessons to learn as a child: work brings you payment for work. David's kids never learned that. Isn't it amazing? I mean even kids on television get an allowance for chores. The idea is out there. Why didn't they pick up on it? Work for pay. How hard is that?

Jack, Cindy and Bryan got all the material and monetary gifts they asked for. Mostly, they asked their mother and she just spent whatever she wanted without any regard for cost. David tells horror stories about her Christmas "budgets." But as I've pointed out to him, it wasn't really her fault at the beginning. She didn't know any better. He held the purse strings and did all the financial planning in the family. No wonder she had no clue. She had no reason to have a clue without having to take responsibility for her actions. After she overspent, she merely got scolded. Not a bad deal for her, but as it turned out, a dreadful deal for the future of their children.

The three of them didn't get a lick of sense as to how to acquire things for themselves. If they couldn't ask their mommy or daddy for something, well, what now? Unfortunately for them, there has never been a what-now moment to deal with. Perhaps if they were left to answer that question, they would have. But instead, they grew up on welfare from dad and they got used to it. I guess it's only natural that all three of them actually ended up as government welfare cases as adults.

Which reminds me of something my friend Ed Hearn recently shared on his Facebook page. He wrote, "The Department of Agriculture, which is responsible for the food stamp program, is boasting of expanding the number of people on food stamps. At the same time, the Department of Agriculture, which has the overall responsibility for our national parks is warning park visitors NOT to feed the animals because it makes them dependent upon others and unable to fend for themselves." Ed also added another comment, "Duh." Now that's an accurate observation of the nationwide prevalence of what I call Daddy Welfare.

Maybe David's kids didn't value work because their mother never had a job, yet spent money like a drunken sailor, and their father always exaggerated about how much money he was making for what he considered very little work. Even now, when he refers back to some of his jobs, he brags about how "easy" they were. Any educated adult who has been out in the work force would chalk up that bragging to, well, bragging. Or if you know the business he's talking about, you understand the work-to-pay ratio is not that of a job that pays by the hour. Some jobs pay for knowledge and the successful application of that knowledge. That's worth a lot and it can't be whittled down to dollars per hour. Children cannot make that distinction. Their father's idea of easy, or doing very little work, appeared that way to him because he was smart, capable and obsessively efficient at his job. He had a talent that was worth a lot of money, regardless of the limited hours he put in. But it was not something he should have bragged about in front of the children. Really. What parent tells their kids not to work hard and take lots of money for little effort? None that I know. And that's not what David meant to do either, but he did. And that helped set up his kids for failure or a life of crime or both.

David didn't realize how his attitude would negatively influence the next generation and how much kids imitate their parents. All three have got their mother down pat. They ask for handouts, drink to excess, chain smoke, and place all the blame on others. He sees that very clearly. He has a harder time seeing the way they imitate him. They're content about not working, yet having a steady stream of income from Daddy Welfare.

So it's clear why they never picked up a work ethic from their parents, but that moral thing should have kicked in when they went to school. They lived in very upscale communities. You can't tell me they had teachers who were just as incompetent as their parents. That's not possible for all three kids for all those years. The teacher in me knows that couldn't happen.

The combination of parents, teachers and church should be able to team up to save even the worst little hellion if they work together and are consistent in their teachings. Oh, there it is. Someone wasn't doing their job and David and Bucky's three children slipped through the cracks. That's what happens when parents come to hate each other more than they love their children.

Jack, Cindy and Bryan were brought up without any organized religion. Although I personally think that's a pretty bad way to bring up a child, I must admit I have friends and relatives who have done the same thing and their kids are moral, productive, educated, successful people with enjoyable lives and many friends. But I still think religion helps. Heck, that's why we Catholics toe the line. We don't want to burn in Hell. Works for me. And the Jews. What my Jewish friends could teach you about guilt! Oy-vey!

Although I didn't have an intense religious upbringing, my parents instilled in me the ideas of faith and fate. It really helps to have faith in moments of despair. It gets me through the tough times. And when the tough times have an unhappy ending, I know it's just fate. It was meant to be and someday that will become clear to me, like when I'm in Heaven and get all the answers. Okay, so I'm making it a little too elementary, but really, it's not rocket science. It's good vs. evil.

Notice that the stories we tell our children all have that common theme: good vs. evil. The Three Little Pigs vs. the Wolf. Little Red Riding Hood vs. the Big Bad Wolf. Gee, wolves get a bad name early. However, many times I've said to Julie that David's kids would be better off if they had been raised by wolves and I still believe that.

Then there's Cinderella and her wicked stepmother. I probably should take another look at that one. Without Dr. Perera, some meds, and membership in a wine club, she probably had a reason to be so wicked. And I don't remember Cinderella's father doing a damn thing for any of those girls. He probably just wrote the checks.

Anyway, my point is that children need to know that good wins out over evil, and if they're good, they'll be winners. It's a simple lesson, but it really resonates with kids.

There was no distinction between right and wrong for David and Bucky's three, just pride in what they could get away with. They learned this by observing their mother as she manipulated David for money and they learned this from David as they listened to how he supposedly ripped off his employers for a wickedly large paycheck. This led all of them to lie, and the lies got bigger as they got older. Too bad for them that the biggest lies have been to themselves. How do you get away from that? They chose alcohol and drugs. And now it's a never-ending cycle.

Here's more of my research:

http://www.bmawellness.com/papers/Addiction_Lies_Rel._html

The first casualty of addiction, like that of war, is the truth. At first the addict merely denies the truth to himself. But as the addiction, like a malignant tumor, slowly and progressively expands and invades more and more of the healthy tissue of his life and mind and world, the addict begins to deny the truth to others as well as to himself.

Lies and addiction fuel a downward spiral at warp speed. But no matter how bad it gets, when daddy's money is there to cushion the crash, they don't get hurt because they never hit bottom. They just keep bouncing over and over. Those of us who have to watch the motion are getting seasick. We want to get off the boat, but we don't want to miss seeing the crash because we know that after the crash there has got to be a massive cleanup and things will get better. We want to see the crash. Please. Someone let them crash so rock bottom could be the starting point for a new life. A better life. It hasn't happened so far. There's been no end to Daddy Welfare, and the downward spiral is halfway to China by now.

Maybe their lack of religion is a good thing. They don't know they're going to Hell. But I do. Faith and fate. Oy-vey!

15

The Bachelor Pads and Don Mattingly

It wasn't long after the divorce and Jack's non-graduate release from high school that he knew he had to get away from the living situation at his mom's house. To hear the boys tell it, no one else really mattered to their mother except Cindy, so why bother?

Jack's first place was a house with a roommate and the roommate's dog. He was near his pizza delivery job and things seemed to be going okay except for the usual requests for money to help keep his car running. I'm sure he regretted drag racing and crashing that brand new one his mom bought him when she got that big settlement check. Now he had to settle for used cars bought with daddy's money.

As time went on, I guess he got more and more confident with his independent lifestyle and he decided to take on a dependent, a dog. He spent some of his hard-earned cash on a purebred Beagle and he named it Don Mattingly, after his favorite New York Yankees baseball player. Now I know there are some Red Sox fans out there who have probably questioned *Donnie Baseball's* (Mattingly's nickname) masculinity at times. The insults you hear in the stands are often amusing and sometimes stupid, but they're all in good fun and they really don't mean anything in the heat of a rivalry. Well, this little Donnie *really* had no balls. It was a girl. Poor little girl getting stuck with both Pizza Boy as a dad and a name like Don Mattingly!

Anyway, as you might have guessed, two dogs in a small house with two young men did not work out for long. I don't really know why, but I'm thinking the roommate decided to make better choices. So Jack went out and got his own apartment. He and Donnie.

Now this was a big financial burden. All the bills were his and you can bet Daddy was called on to help more than once. During this time, the money didn't bother me as much as worrying about the dog. I hate it when people who can't take care of themselves get pets. Morons! It killed me to wait it out. I knew we'd get the dog eventually and I was concerned about the bad habits we'd have to break from her puppyhood.

I don't actually remember how long this apartment lasted, but I'm pretty sure it was less than a year before Pizza Boy decided he needed to move again. I've blocked out the reason for this move too because the big deal was that the new apartment he found would not take a dog. Finally. We already had my two cats and a 126-pound Akita, acquired in my brother's divorce, and David gently suggested to me that we should take Donnie too. Of course I told him yes, but I also made it clear that once we took the dog, she was ours. I would not give her back. She needed people who would keep her clean and healthy, get her nails cut and pay attention to her. That was not Pizza Boy.

I'm happy to report that Donnie lived a long and comfortable life, even retiring to Florida with us to spend her golden years in the sunshine, often riding around the neighborhood with us in our golf cart. She was a blessing and we have Pizza Boy to thank.

For some reason I seem to remember as financial, this non-dog apartment didn't work out either and Jack was looking for any solution that wouldn't lead him back to his mother's. His father's cousin Emma, whom David lived with after the divorce, had plenty of room in her house. Her mother, David's Aunt Anna, had since died. But Jack was not David and I warned Emma that he would not be the perfect roommate for her. Despite my warning (does anyone ever listen to me?), she said he could move in.

He liked it there, paying minimal rent, with no bills and there was always food in the fridge. Emma worked full-time days and Jack delivered his pizzas at night and on weekends. It seemed like a good solution for both. Emma had a dog and she was happy that it got twice the attention now. But this stop on the bachelor pad tour didn't last long either.

16

Retail Therapy

I left my husband a note. He had already left for the golf course.

Went shopping. Don't worry.

Won't spend more than $2,600

and "*I'll pay you back.*"

Love, K

Yikes. I felt guilty for just writing the note. How was I actually going to follow through with it? It was a desperate attempt to get my husband's attention. Not because he had been neglecting me, but because he has forever been neglecting his duties as a parent and this was going to be my first attempt at pointing this out by hitting him in the wallet. Besides, I made close to $60,000 a year. I could actually afford a small shopping spree without his knowledge or permission. But we are both so frugal that I knew he'd take my note as a personal attack and he'd feel like I was draining *his* bank account rather than *ours*. That was my mission: make him feel the pinch.

For the fourth time in the past six years, Jack asked his father to help him buy a used car, always promising, "I'll pay you back."

Always failing to keep that promise. And once again, my husband agreed, forking over $2,600 for a heap of metal that Jack would likely run into the ground or crash within the year.

Now I ask you, how can a 30-year old boy (yes, boy) who lives with, and off, his father's lovely, selfless cousin Emma, and doesn't have any expenses, not have $2,600 for a used car. Gee, I wonder. He has a job. In fact, he's had the same job ever since he was 16, delivering pizzas. Must be some sort of record. Fourteen years as a pizza delivery boy. Six more and he qualifies for a pension, right? Regardless of how much it pays, he does bring in money, tips too. In fact he's always been paid "under the table." So no one, not even Uncle Sam, gets a slice of his pizza pie. Yes, 30 years old and he's never paid taxes because he's never been officially employed.

So as Woodward and Bernstein would say, "Let's follow the money." From pizza customer's wallet to Jack's pocket and then, well, let's see. Jack was both a heavy drinker and a pothead (this was before his diabetes diagnosis which made him stop drinking but not puffing). He's also lost a lot of weight lately over a rather short period of time. Hmm. Could it be vanishing in a cloud of inhaled dust? Well wherever it's going, it's not going to pay back his father for any of the other three used cars he's bought him.

You'd think Dad would have caught on by now. Maybe he has. Maybe it's just that Land of Denial vacation he takes from time to time. He's happy there.

So off I go on my attention-getting spending spree. First stop, Steinmart. I love that store because the prices are so reasonable. Well, that was the wrong mindset. I bought some designer J. Lo sunglasses and a couple of nice leather wallets, but it added up to less than $100 and I needed to find a more efficient way to throw away $2,600.

It was surprisingly difficult to spend money just for the sake of spending money. I didn't need anything and I'm not used to buying for no reason. I guess I was raised differently than David's kids. I learned to work to earn money and not to spend too much because it's important to have some kind of savings for a rainy day. Whereas David's brats enjoyed having money rain down on them whenever they whined.

Next stop, a swimsuit store. I could justify spending money there. After all, we have several pools in our community and I play water volleyball twice a week. The chlorine in the indoor pool is tough on bathing suits. I need several of them so I won't look washed out and faded during the big games. But I was still working against myself. Justifying a purchase? I was supposed to be throwing away $2,600 like Pizza Boy did. Yet I really couldn't do it. I needed to *justify* it.

I failed miserably with the swimsuits because everything was *on sale*. Really? A swimsuit sale in Orlando. Are they kidding? This is an item on which to make profits year-round in Florida. I wondered if retailers had gone mad? It just wasn't my day. I was trying to help increase sales and the Retail Gods were against me. Less than $200 dropped here and I had to get on my way to bigger and better things.

Bigger. That's it. I had to think big. What big item could I buy that would get me closer to my $2,600 goal? Outdoor furniture. With a lanai to fill, you can't have enough outdoor furniture.

I drove out to furniture row in Orlando and stopped at the first outdoor furniture store I saw. I went up to a saleswoman and asked to see the most expensive furniture she had. She gave me a funny look, but led me to it. I decided on a couple of chairs with a matching table.

She asked if I wanted the chairs to rock. I asked if that would cost more than the non-rocking chairs. She said yes. I said, "Yes."

She asked if I wanted them to swivel too. I asked if that cost more. She said yes. I said, "Yes."

She asked if I wanted the high backs or low backs. I asked which cost more. She said the high backs. I said, "The high backs."

She asked if I wanted the lifetime guarantee on the finish. I asked if it cost more. She said yes. I said, "Yes."

She asked if I wanted the round table or the square. I asked which cost more. She said they were the same price. I said, "Pick one. Surprise me." She chose the round one.

She asked if I wanted them delivered. I said only if it costs more. She said it depended on the mileage. I said, "Fine. Deliver them by way of Cleveland." She laughed.

And as she wrote up the sale, I told her the story of my spending spree and she seemed to enjoy it. But alas, I was still about $1,100 shy of my goal. What to do, what to do?

The internet! I should have thought of that earlier. I'm a master at internet shopping for gifts. Now I had permission to buy myself some gifts. Well, I didn't need any personal items, clothing or jewelry. Besides, David rarely notices new purchases of either. I needed to look for something that would stare him in the face every day with a subtle message that screams out, *"Look at me! Look at me! Your wife paid a ridiculous price for the likes of me to reside in your home because you don't have the cajones to be a good father and raise men instead of 3-year-old girls."*

Found it. Cabinet knobs for the kitchen. I had actually been shopping for cabinet knobs recently at Home Depot and I found some lovely pieces. Most were priced between $3 and $6. Some local cabinet stores had a few more expensive ones which I remembered from a shopping trip weeks ago. I didn't consider those because of the higher prices. After all, they're just knobs used to open kitchen cabinets, like a car is used for transportation. I drive a Hyundai. I've never been able to justify splurging on a utility item. (Geez, there's that "j" word again.) That was then. My mission now was to find the most expensive cabinet knobs in the world, 22 little works of art that would make visitors to my kitchen "ooh" and "aah" on their first and all subsequent visits. Fourteen of those 22 knobs would be screwed in at just about David's eye level. Perfect. The others would be at the level of his missing cajones. Perfectly ironic.

I found them on a website from a company in Seattle. Lovely red ceramic knobs with yellow and green flecks and a small gold medallion in the center. The perfect way to open my 22 cabinet doors and a bargain at $27.50 each. Thank goodness they weren't *on sale*. That's $605 when you do the math. And it was such a ridiculous amount of money to pay for cabinet knobs that I no longer felt the need to spend the rest of the $2,600. I felt validated in my little plot of revenge.

When David came home from the golf course, he told me how foolish I was to leave him that note about spending $2,600. I smiled. He asked me what I bought. I told him sunglasses, wallets, bathing suits, furniture and 22 kitchen cabinet knobs.

He said, "You didn't spend $2,600 did you?"

I said, "Of course not. But I did go a little overboard on the cabinet knobs."

He said, "That's okay. I know you were mad about another car for Jack, but he needs it to work."

Later that evening, as David was opening a kitchen cabinet, he said, "How much did you spend on the cabinet knobs?"

I told him, "Twenty-seven dollars and 50 cents."

"That's not much," he said.

Then I got in the last word, "Each."

It was a very quiet night.

17

Nationwide is On Your Side

The phone rang this morning.

"Is David there?"

David is always in bed sleeping at 9 a.m., so I tried to help, considering it sounded like a typical marketing call. No one who knows him would ever call David until after 11 a.m.

"May I ask who's calling?" I said. I was in the bedroom and David could hear me through his slumber.

"Rona, from Nationwide Insurance," she answered.

"We don't have Nationwide Insurance," I said.

"Yes we do," David said. "Give me the phone."

This ought to be good, I thought.

"We" turned out to be Bryan and Jack, alias "David" to the Nationwide Insurance Company. Seems Daddy took out their car insurance in his name even though they were ages 36 and 24 at the time. They promised to make the payments. Oops. I could tell all of this from David's end of the phone conversation. What I couldn't tell was if they actually needed that car insurance right now. Was there an accident?

He didn't say a word when he got off the phone.

Kerry: Was anyone hurt or killed?

David: Nothing happened.

Kerry: No accident?

David: No.

Kerry: So you're just paying the insurance for them?

David: Well, I pay Bryan's while he's in school.

(Taking 2 fucking classes, so he says, and not doing another damn thing like working, since he actually flunked out of school in his junior year, which was well over a year ago.)

Kerry: And Jack?

David: I only pay it when he can't.

I thought, what the hell does that mean? Always? But I didn't say a word. My look was deadly and he knew exactly what I was thinking. Unfortunately for me, we were long past the days when I was able to make pizza delivery career jokes out loud. I miss those days. I ought to put them all in a book. I have loads of them.

Unfortunately for David, the day before Rona from Nationwide called, he made a big fuss about my current "spending spree." And while it's true I had made some purchases over the past week or so, I'd hardly label it a "spree." I mean it's not like I was buying more cabinet knobs.

The nearby Liz Claiborne Outlet was going out of business. Add it up: Liz + outlet + closing = bargains. I bought three white cotton long-sleeved shirts for $36. A wardrobe basic and a sensible purchase. It's rare to get Liz for $12 each. Even David knows that.

The previous Saturday I bought two necklaces and two place mats at our annual Village Craft Festival. Total cost: $33. I didn't break the bank on that day either.

Also, that week I took one of my former students out to lunch to celebrate her venture into the college ranks. David asked me to bring a take-out lunch home for him from the same restaurant. The two lunches and take-out, with tip, came to $26.

Okay, so I've got a "spending spree" of $95 going on. That's what he made a big fuss about the day before Nationwide Rona's call. But I'm not through. He was stupid enough to continue to *jokingly* badger me about my spending that very afternoon, after Nationwide Rona's call.

I went to the local Walmart to pick up a few groceries, including bread. When David shops, he always gets the generic whole wheat loaf that's $1.88. I prefer the Nature's Valley whole wheat loaf that's $2.52. If you're like David, you've already done the math and realize that I overspend for bread by sixty-four cents a loaf. But David eats a lot more bread than I do, so unless I'm planning a week of sandwiches for myself, I usually buy his bread and bank that sixty-four cents. But on this day, the shelf of cheap bread was empty, so I broke open the bank and shopped off the top shelf.

As I'm unpacking the groceries on the kitchen counter he says, "You got *your* bread. That's 64 cents more. How are you gonna make that up?"

Now I know he was just kidding. And on any other day I would have laughed, but not on this day. Not when the day started with Rona from Nationwide asking for a car insurance payment for cars that were not ours. I had warned him before not to kid about money until he stopped throwing away $600 a month on Pizza Boy's rent and more on his "expenses." Now I find out there's car insurance for the two cars we *gave* to the two deadbeats.

So I calmly said, "I can easily find an extra $600 a month in our budget."

My idiot husband makes the mistake of asking "Where?"

"Some liquor store in Connecticut," I replied.

It was pretty quiet for the rest of the day. Except for me humming the jingle, "Nationwide is on your side."

18

An Email for Evidence

Hi Julie,

Just sitting here with a glass of wine and my laptop. Taking the night (and day) off from talking to David because today I found out he's paying the car insurance for both boys. Yes, car insurance for the cars we gave them.

Geez, when I think of how I learned to budget for car payments. They'll never learn that. Hell, they'll never learn anything.

And for the record, I was totally against giving those cars to them. David did that on his own. I don't think anyone should give a car to a pothead or a drunk. Please keep this email to be used in court for any upcoming vehicular manslaughter cases. It should get me off the hook.

Kerry

Hey Ker,

None of Kevin's 3 girls own cars. They have them. But he owns all of them.

Currently, Trisha is still not talking to us. Terry lives in a shelter because she says it's cheaper than paying rent and Tracy is still living with her mother.

Kevin got a letter from Terry this week, addressing him as "Mr. Winston" and requesting no more contact with him. He wrote her back telling her he would honor her request and he signed it, "Mr. Winston."

Mrs. Winston

Dear Mrs. Winston,

Thanks for making me laugh with the tales from your husband's young 'uns. Aint' it grand to have such precious kin folk?

Ms. Kendall

19

A House for Pizza Boy

David went out for awhile and when he came back he had a written list of houses in our area that were for sale cheap. A written list with prices. Not houses in our lovely 55-plus community, but outside the gates, where he usually doesn't drive alone because he gets lost and he doesn't speak enough Spanish to ask for directions. Not that he ever would, ask for directions I mean. But this time he was on a mission, so he must have really tried hard to navigate, drive and search because he found his way around. He covered a good amount of territory, according to the long list.

We had talked about an investment property over the years and always decided against it after weighing the pros and cons. The biggest con is that David can't fix anything and I'm always working and don't have the time to tend to one house, never mind two. So all the maintenance would cost us a ton of money and we'd be rolling the dice on finding good repair people. David also feared the type of renters we might get and how much wear and tear there would be on our investment. Overall, it's just not for us. We have enough to deal with. So when he showed me this list, I reminded him of that. I also reminded him that Kevin and Julie had rental properties for awhile and they advised against it too. It just wasn't worth the trouble, according to Kevin. And Julie, well, her renter stories were topped only by her stepdaughter stories, so I was convinced. I reminded him of all that. David wholeheartedly agreed, when I stopped talking long enough for him to get in a few words. I was pleased, but confused. So then I made the mistake of asking, "What in the hell are you pricing cheap houses for?"

"It's not for us. It's for Jack," he said matter-of-factly. He was keeping his voice low and his emotions in check, hoping I'd do the same. Good plan, but only in theory. At this time, Jack was an uneducated 34-year-old pizza deliverer and I was about to blow if David was serious about buying the *kid* a house anywhere, especially in our neighborhood.

I'm sure the look on my face said it all. Yet he stupidly, but quickly, went on to explain, "He'll never be able to get anything in Connecticut."

Luckily for David, I was busy cooking for a dinner party. I tried to stay calm and I purposely steered clear of the razor sharp Cutco cleaver in the knife block, but I couldn't hold my tongue or stifle my sarcastic wit.

"Perhaps getting a real job so he could pay his own rent would be an admirable first step to getting *anything anywhere*. Why not start him there?" I said.

David stormed off in a huff. In just minutes, our friends arrived for dinner.

Our kitchen is open to the family room, and as I'm cooking I hear David telling everyone about his wonderful afternoon of bargain shopping, looking for houses for his son because he'd "like to bring him down here because he'll never get anything up there. I could buy him a house with a pool for under $100,000." True, David could buy him a house with a pool, but why should he? Did your parents buy you a house with a pool? Did you even expect them to?

More steam was coming out of me than out of the pots and pans. I was already planning my own escape with well over the $100,000 that I would get if we split up. That would certainly put a damper on his second-house plan. Truly, he must have gotten heat stroke out there in the Florida sun. I did not sign up for having an under-employed 34-year-old attached to my husband or his wallet. In fact, one of the reasons David wanted to move over a thousand miles away from Connecticut was to get away from his three dreadful adult children. We actually discussed it. He didn't want to be near them. He knew they'd still bother us by phone, but he was glad to be able to put some distance between us. Did he forget?

When Jack was very sick and found to be diabetic the previous year, David also wanted to bring him down to Florida. That time, he suggested we take him in to live with us. All I had to say was, "If you do, I'll leave you and take your money." It was that easy. He never mentioned it again.

Of course David knew I wasn't serious about the threat to leave him, but he also knew I *was* serious about not taking in Pizza Boy to live with us. For weeks afterward, he jokingly mentioned my threat to friends of ours who told me right in front of him that I did the right thing for both of us. He knew it too. He was grateful that I stopped the train wreck before he started it.

So now, with the house shopping, was he daring me to put my foot down again? Was this plan designed to take the load off him and make me the bad guy? Did he think I'd start to feel guilty? Certainly not for a deadbeat man-child who has never had a real job and never lifted a finger to help himself or anyone else. Not even my Catholic guilt would factor into this episode.

When Jack remained in Connecticut throughout his illness after the diabetes diagnosis, Daddy ended up renting an apartment for him and paying for it for 10 months until Pizza Boy was back on his feet and sprinting across town to deliver those pies. Oh, and daddy didn't go back to Connecticut to do it. He did it all online and by phone so he wouldn't actually have to be there in the midst of the drama.

You might be wondering why Pizza Boy needed an apartment at that time. After all, he was living in cousin Emma's big house. There was plenty of room. Well, as he found out, even Emma has her breaking point.

Gracious, patient, tolerant, naïve Emma got a huge wake-up call when Bryan came to stay with them for a few weeks after his first year in college. His mother didn't seem to have any room for him and he didn't want to come to Florida to stay with us. All of a sudden both boys couldn't hide their drinking and pot-smoking behavior like one of them did. Emma grew a set of steel balls and threw them both out. I was so proud of her and told her so many times, hoping to prevent any backsliding on her part. But I found out she's a strong woman, stronger than her cousin David. She cut the ties and never looked back.

I celebrated a little victory on my part too. I held back and never said "I told you so." Even though I really, really wanted to. She actually beat me to it. She voluntarily told me she should have listened to me years before. I had warned her that David's kids weren't always the well-behaved little group she saw at Christmas. And now she knew. She and I are pretty good friends now. Comrades. I guess we have a couple of drunk potheads to thank for that. I've learned to look for the good in every situation. There it is.

Several months after Emma threw the ungrateful boys out, Pizza Boy wanted to come back to get the air conditioner she once promised to give him. While he was living there, she kept a key hidden outside and he expected it to still be there. It wasn't. She *really* didn't want him back for *any* reason. When he didn't find the key, he called his daddy, who of course was 1,300 miles away from his current problem. Maybe a call to Emma, politely asking for the air conditioner, should have been his next step. But no, he invaded our lives in Florida again to complain about not being able to break into Emma's house in Connecticut. So David called Emma at work, who confirmed she no longer left a key because she didn't want either of his sons in her house. But she also said Pizza Boy was welcome to get the extra air conditioner when she was home to give it to him. So David called him, and before he could relay Emma's message, I heard him say, "You did? You probably shouldn't have done that. But she said you could have it."

Pizza Boy took the initiative and broke in through a window. Illegally, of course. But hey, this was the first evidence of problem-solving that I had ever seen from him. I was slightly impressed. Perhaps some brain cells were surviving the toxicity of their environment.

David didn't seem to think the kid did anything wrong, even though I pointed out the breaking-and-entering angle of the incident. "After all," he said, "she said he could have it." And now he did.

However, that's not the end of this story. For the rest of the day and into the evening, David was upset at Emma because he said she caused the whole problem. His rationale: "Emma said he could have the air conditioner. She always left the key for him. How would Jack know she took it away? I can't believe she did that. He would not have broken in if she left the key."

And that my friends, is enabling in a nutshell. If only she left the damn key out there so the pothead could return for a free air conditioner and not have to break in through a window.

As for the end of the house-shopping story, our dinner guests could feel the tension between us as David outlined his second-home plan. They were smart enough not to encourage him and talked up the disadvantages of buying income property that would generate no income. That was the bottom line for a numbers guy like David. No matter what he bought, it would ultimately be a black hole and he didn't need Stephen Hawking to explain this one.

20

Emails on a Summer Night

Hi Julie,

Hope things are going well over there in Mississippi. Here's my update:

Pizza boy has moved from the $600 a month apartment he couldn't afford into a $700 apartment he can't afford. It belongs to his friend Anthony (or Anthony's dad) and they used to get $1,000 rent but they're giving it to Pizza Boy for less. I'd take bets on how long that's gonna last. A smoker who doesn't clean up after himself with a friend for a landlord who will probably see the apartment getting trashed over time. Yep, that's a sure bet.

David started a fight with me today after I told him I was taking the car to Walmart for an oil change. He said I always overpay. That means, "Stop taking the car to where it's convenient and look for a coupon/bargain/sale." So I calmly told him I pay for convenience because I don't have the time, like he does, to run all over town for a bargain. He said there's a place in Haines City that does it for $17. So I asked him how he'd even know that, since he never takes the car in for *any* service. He insisted he went there for an oil change. But I know I've done all the oil changes on our car. So I kept at him, only to discover it was Bryan's car he took in for a fucking oil change. God forbid he should do something to make my life easier. Needless to say, he'll be taking *our* car in for an oil change next week if he doesn't want the engine to seize up. I spent the afternoon shopping and not answering my phone.

Tonight I told him I don't know how Bucky survived 18 years with him because we're not even going to make the 13-year mark because he's driving me up the fucking wall with his nickel and diming, yet throwing away all kinds of money on the pothead and the drunks.

Several weeks ago Bryan insisted he needed to go to rehab. Now he says he doesn't. Instead, he's going back to school. Yeah, that's a scene I'm glad to be 1,300 miles away from. Tuition well spent, no doubt.

Our new cell phone service is AT&T. I hate it, but it's free to friends and family and of course David also got Pizza Boy and Drunk Boy new AT&T phones. Because of my schedule, I've usually got the cell phone. David is too cheap to get one too. So you can imagine how often my cell phone rings with their calls. I've set the ringer with a don't-answer tune.

Just had to vent. I know, get used to it, find a way to deal with it, or get out. My plan is to deal with it and keep venting in writing to add to my book file. What is it they say about that which doesn't kill us, makes us stronger? Yeah, right. I don't feel strong. I'm drained.

Kerry

Ker,

So sorry you're having a rough spot. I've been there.

Kids and money are what ALL couples fight about. I remember years ago my brother's girlfriend Betsy went to Los Angeles to visit a college friend who was marrying a big time Hollywood producer. She stayed at their house in Beverly Hills, went to Rodeo Drive for the wedding dress fitting, Tiffany's to pick up the rings, and when they got home, Betsy said he bitched her out because she bought Diet Coke at Ralph's and they had it on sale somewhere else. I don't know what that's about or how you *fix* it but I know you're not alone.

Julie

21

Girls Just Wanna Have....
Who the Hell Knows?

With four stepdaughters between us, you'd think Julie or I would have scored big with at least one of them. After all, we've been role models for other girls. The success we've had with newsroom interns, students and other young women who have worked with us can be documented. We've got references. To paraphrase Sally Field, "They like us. They really like us."

We have many female friends too. Close ones, casual acquaintances and old friends from school. We know how to cultivate both inner and outer circles. We appreciate them. So what went so freakishly wrong with these four girls who should have gone out of their way to get into our circles?

Julie and I met their fathers long after the dissolution of their parents' marriages. We didn't break up the *happy* homes. We also had demanding full-time jobs during at least the first ten years of marriage, so we didn't take up all of their fathers' time. And how about the energy we put into the birthdays and holidays? Did they not see it? Did they think their fathers automatically became expert shoppers, cooks and hosts once they got married again?

I've already mentioned Julie's ability to super shop. She put that to use for Kevin's girls on many occasions. There were three or more weddings for each of them, parties for the babies they had, birthdays for them and their husbands and children. There was a ton of gifts. It was Julie's time and energy that got them chosen, bought, wrapped and delivered. Their father didn't lift a finger, except to pay the bills of course. And that seemed to be the only part of the gift-giving that they acknowledged. "Thanks Dad."

It took many years before Julie stopped. It just wasn't worth it. Taking the time to go to the mall and pick out the perfect gift did not make sense when you didn't even get a "thank you." From that point on, they all got checks from Kevin and the tables were turned. He didn't get any "thank yous" either. In fact, he actually got demands for more gifts.

When it was time for a grandchild's birthday, any one of the three girls would approach him with her plans for the party. They'd ask him to pay for it, or buy a huge expensive cake and some big gift which they, no doubt, would take credit for giving their own kid. They expected the financial support and over-the-top birthday shopping for their child, instead of realizing and appreciating that Grandpa would come through with a gift on his own without being directed.

I used to Christmas shop year-round for Cindy and the boys. In fact, I did theme shopping. That's where all the gifts have a common theme, elaborate color-coordinated wrapping, and are chosen especially for what the recipient is currently interested in. It's actually fun to do, but it takes up a whole lot of time. Those were the days before internet shopping. And did they appreciate it? Well, I must admit, I think the boys did. But Cindy? She seemed to go out of her way not to say "thank you." So I eventually got mad as hell and decided not to take it anymore either.

Before Christmas one year, I told David he was now in charge of gifts for his own kids. You would have thought I hacked off their right arms with a chainsaw. He was incensed. *What? Not buy gifts for my kids? What's the matter with you, woman?* Well, maybe that wasn't his actual response, but that's what he meant when he said, "Why not?"

I chose the non-confrontational route and told him I was really busy around the holidays with all that decorating and cookie baking. And I had loads of projects to grade for my students. I threw a few more things in the mix and pointed out that he had a lot more free time to shop and clinched the deal with, "And wouldn't they just love to know you actually went out and shopped for them?"

What a Christmas that was! With my gifts, even Cindy couldn't hide her enthusiasm when she pulled a ribbon and opened a box, despite her lack of thanks. With David's gifts, she couldn't hide her bewilderment. I thoroughly enjoyed watching her open each gift bag. David didn't seem to have any extra time for wrapping or bows, so he used gift bags. She got hair brushes and combs, a mirror, some body lotions and sprays, a manicure kit and nail polish and, well, you get the idea. He sort of theme shopped too. The day before Christmas he scoured the local drug store for what was left on the shelves. One-stop shopping. Gotta hand it to him. It was quick. He didn't let gift shopping take over his schedule like I used to. No wonder he didn't fully appreciate my time problem. He man-shopped!

I'm sorry to say that was the one and only year he man-shopped. From that point on, he just wrote checks, rationalizing that the kids knew what they wanted better than he did. Ya think?

So our time and energy and thoughtfulness didn't get Julie and I liked by the girls. Our delightful manners as hostesses did not get us in the fold. Our skills in providing wonderful meals didn't make a bit of difference to them. And if they only knew how many times we made their fathers consider them before flying off the handle or doing something that would even slightly offend them, well, that probably wouldn't have gotten us anywhere either. They used all their energy to be stubborn, unwelcoming and ungrateful.

Considering that these girls have gone from teenagers to adults in their 30s and 40s over the course of our marriages, you might wonder why the relationships never straightened out. Or maybe you already see it clearly like we do. These girls never left their teens. They were given all they asked for by their mothers. Their behaviors were tolerated and financed by their fathers. They never had to make an adult decision, so they didn't. They became masters at manipulation. They turned to mommy or daddy and got validated or bailed out. No questions asked or answered. The girls never had to explain their behavior to anyone, not even themselves. They never had to grow up.

Being grown women ourselves, we knew where this would lead. Nowhere. They were on a hamster wheel, going around and around. Year after year, there was no progress. Failed relationships, loss of child custody, car repossessions, bankruptcies, arrests and therapy. Never-ending therapy. But nothing actually broke any of them for the longest time until Tracy's fatal overdose. And even that may have been an accident.

Their disregard for education or for those who have it was astonishing to me. I'm from a world where we look up to smart people and try to learn from them.

I was also amazed by their feelings of entitlement which led to failure whenever any of them actually found a job.

Trisha once got fired for embezzling over $10,000. Considering her drama-queen lifestyle, you might think she needed it to feed and clothe her children, or to pay the rent. Any of those choices could be exactly why she was desperate enough to steal from her employer. But she didn't spend any of it on her kids or her bills. She took that $10,000 to a fine jewelry store and bought herself a Rolex watch. Priorities.

David's Cindy is quite the job-hopper. She has dabbled in so many fields that she could probably offer guidance to the unemployed, if she were ever sober. Pizza Boy has taken her in to his place of business a few times to act as a server. But that never works out for long. She'll eventually come to work drunk, embarrass him and get fired. And even when she's not working at his current pizza parlor, she often pays him a visit, while drunk, and he has to deliver her home while on his pizza route.

Cindy is very much her mother's daughter in the employment department. Bucky went through a series of jobs after she ran out of money. The $650,000 settlement, child support and alimony didn't last long. She eventually stopped drinking and found work in the offices of several medical businesses. She got fired a few times, but seemed to learn enough about the business to always get hired by someone else. Over the past few years, she's been sober and stable in the same job in a specialty department of an area hospital. And she has done her best to send Cindy out to apply for jobs with local doctors.

Once Cindy told her father she went on an interview and was offered a job in a medical office for $14 an hour. Not bad for someone with no college education, skills or references. She then told him she didn't take it because the boss said she could be fired "anytime for doing something wrong." She didn't like this idea.

As David retold the story to me, he said, "Do you think it's right that a guy should have said this to her in an interview?" Did he think she really went on a job interview?

Duh. No references, extremely overweight, smells of nicotine, glassy-eyed, uneducated and she's never held a job for more than a couple of months. If the story was true, I think that guy was desperate and hedging his bets. Why should she be choosey when he wasn't?

In that same conversation with my husband, he also told me that Cindy said her mother once got fired for "no reason." I guess David believed this story too because he said to me, "That's not right to get fired for no reason." I love David too much to make his gullibility work for me but, really. Bucky has stolen, lied, and committed forgery to get credit cards with his name on them. This was all *during* their marriage. How could she be trusted to keep her hands out of the cash drawer in an office? Chances are, if she was fired, it wasn't for "no reason."

It's obvious that all of the stepdaughters knew they needed to work at some time, even if just to fill their time. But there was never any evidence of them working toward something like financial security, a promotion, a better job or, God forbid, a career. And they often turned to their parents for help in getting in the door. I don't know how many connections Bucky used up, but David used up plenty of favors over the years for both Cindy and Pizza Boy.

This brings to mind a book I was required to read before I started as a high school teacher in Polk County, Florida. It was about classes of people defined by their economic status. The thing that really stuck with me was the observation that kids raised in affluent families see things differently. They have a plan to succeed which involves getting into the best schools and country clubs and staying connected with the best families. It's who you know, not what you know. They've never known what it's like to need money because they've always had it.

Kids raised in poverty often have the idea that to get ahead they need to score. They think they have to hit the lottery or do something like sell drugs in order to get cash. They're desperate to get out of their poor circumstances and they'll take chances to get money.

The middle class, the blue-collar kids, work hard and study hard because they see that as their ticket to a better life. Their parents drill the idea into them. So they take charge and try to become successful and achieve something on their own. They want their parents to be proud.

Now I know these are only generalizations. But I see them in my own extended family among all three groups. Rich kids can be just as disadvantaged as poor kids. It's essentially true unless someone thinks outside the box and goes rogue.

Julie broke out of her upper class roots with her independent spirit. No one works harder than she does. Kevin rose from a childhood of poverty to his current affluence by working hard and educating himself about the business world. David broke out of a lower-middle-class upbringing, first with athletic talent, and then with the college education he got with his sports scholarships. Me, I've always felt like a middle-class diva. I knew I could do anything as long as I was given time to work at it. Four successful people with one common denominator: We know the value of hard work.

Kevin and David have not passed that on. I wonder if Julie and I would have passed it on if we had children of our own. I'd like to think we would have for one reason: We're not stupid! The frustration is maddening.

22

Rescue Me, 'Cause We've Lost #3

"If there is a God, he's got a whole shitload of explaining to do."

– Denis Leary as Tommy Gavin
Episode 1 of Rescue Me

For seven television seasons, ending on September 11, 2011, I was hooked on *Rescue Me*, the series created by Denis Leary, which followed the lives of New York City firefighters after the tragedy of 9-11. Watching it was like being on an emotional roller coaster. Death, alcoholism, adultery, homosexuality, lying, cheating, stealing, life. Was it a tragic comedy or a comic tragedy? The Internet Movie Data Base lists it under both drama and comedy. Either way, I know I laughed during every episode and always at the most politically incorrect moments.

That's what I suspect it's like for someone else to hear or read about my life and Julie's, with the stepkids who were not parented, just financed. She and I had to develop coping skills. Mine were rooted in humor. If I don't find a way to laugh about something, I'll just keep crying. I knew it wasn't the politically correct thing to do, but hey, neither is cannibalism. It's just a survival tool.

It's not like I could do anything about the kids. It was either, "Get out now," like Julie said, or stay and watch and try to minimize the collateral damage to my marriage. Julie and I both threw ourselves into work, changing careers and striving for success in several fields. Somewhere along the line, we each hit an emotional wall, climbed over it, and tried to make the most of our lives with help from each other, therapists, alcohol and anti-depressants. Sometimes getting over the hurdles involved unloading on our respective therapists, then crying to each other on the phone while washing down those anti-depressants with a good cabernet. You'll have to find what works for you.

I really tried hard to rescue Bryan. He came to live with us before the start of the seventh grade. We wanted to get him away from his mother's and sister's estrogen-fueled alcoholic environment earlier, but our lawyer (yes, David's real estate guy who did a less-than-stellar job with the divorce and made that big mistake with the breathalyzer advice) told us it would be very costly and almost impossible to win custody from his mother. However, he did suggest that we make her an offer. He was familiar with what she valued and smart enough to suggest we use it against her. David crunched the numbers and figured $25,000 would be less than what he'd pay in child support and other expenses until Bryan turned 18, so the lawyer put it in writing and David presented Bucky with the deal. She didn't have the sense to crunch the numbers. She saw the bottom line and signed it. Sold for 25 grand! We were happy to be able to rescue him, but it was a sad day too, knowing that Bryan's own mother valued cash more than her own son.

The first few years were enlightening. It was more of an adjustment for me than Bryan. I couldn't believe the lack of parenting skills in my otherwise intelligent husband. I tried not to interfere, hoping David would step up to the plate and start parenting, considering he had to do it full-time now. But nothing changed. It was as if Bryan was still the Wednesday night and weekend visitor that David wanted to entertain. There was no bedtime, no chores, no set times for homework or television, no supervision of t.v. viewing or internet use. It was like watching a teenage babysitter who was trying to get the kid to like him. I was probably no help. Not wanting to be the wicked stepmother, I let it go on for longer than I should have.

Eventually, I started to assign chores to Bryan like cleaning his room and his own bathroom. Bryan seemed okay with that, however he was a typical kid and had to be reminded hundreds of times. I was okay with that. David wasn't. There were many times I would come home from school to find David scrubbing the toilet in Bryan's bathroom. He didn't want to hear me nagging Bryan, so that was his solution. I tried to point out that the best solution would be for *him* to give Bryan some chores, including lawn work, snow shoveling and washing the car from time to time. But no. David did it all. And it was not a battle I was willing to fight anymore, at least not after the first couple of years when I was worn out from fighting about it. It's as if David was afraid to give Bryan a task he wouldn't like and therefore wouldn't like his father. Whatever the reason, it served to make Bryan irresponsible and lazy, just like his brother and sister. Everything was done for him.

As Bryan got older, we had what I call the "typical teenage problems" with parties, drinking, smoking, pot, whatever. That's when I stepped up. Once I smelled cigarette smoke in his room, and he lied to me about it, that was it. I blew up. It was a Friday afternoon and he was leaving to go to his mother's for a rare weekend visit and he couldn't leave fast enough for me. David wasn't home and without calling to warn him, I took the door off Bryan's room. The kid was going to have to earn the right to privacy in our house. When Bucky brought him back on Sunday, I told him he'd get the door back when he deserved privacy and stopped lying. It was our house and cigarette smoking was not allowed inside. Bucky was appalled. I don't know if it was the missing door that bothered her or the fact that she always reeked of cigarette smoke and it wasn't a problem for her. She said if I didn't put the door back on, she'd take Bryan back to her place. I opened the front door and ushered them out.

Bryan would miss school the next day if she took him back to Fairfield. Bryan didn't like to miss school at this point, so I didn't think he'd follow her like a puppy, but he did.

He had second thoughts by the time he got back to her place though. He called his father and asked him to pick him up. Of course David drove all the way down there to get him. While waiting for them, I was thinking that Bryan realized I was right and he would apologize as soon as he walked in. Wrong. The not-so-little monster worked on David all the way home and David *told me* to put the door back on. Yep, David *told me* to do it because he wouldn't know how to work a door hinge pin if his life depended on it. He's the type of guy who pays people to do things rather than trying to do something himself. Whoa! That probably set a bad example for the kids too. I don't remember exactly what I said to him, but it wasn't nice. I think I told him where he could put, or shove, the door.

It took two days before David got a neighbor to help him put the door back on. In those two days, there was no discussion of smoking, smoking in the house, following any rules, lying to us or anything that prompted me to make that door disappear. In other words, no lessons came out of all that family upheaval. There was only appeasement of the kid who was turning into a juvenile delinquent before our very eyes. I felt like I was the only one who noticed and it hurt to watch.

The spring of Bryan's junior year of high school, things went downhill fast. We mistakenly trusted him to stay home for a week, with my father, the very observant retired police officer, looking in on him daily. We made another trip to Florida for the closing of the new house that we weren't going to move into until Bryan graduated from high school. My father didn't sound right on the phone when I called. It was as if he was trying *not* to tell me something.

When we got home, I found several things out of place. Small things, but they were noticeable. I also found some jewelry in my bedroom and it wasn't mine. It was too cheap to belong to a grown woman, not that I'd ever suspect David of something like that. He already had too much to handle without adding an affair to the mix. Besides, it was an adolescent girl's jewelry. So then I checked the liquor bottles, which I had marked before we left. I'm not stupid. I was a high school teacher. They were way down from my marks.

Despite being exhausted after driving 21 hours from Florida, I told David he needed to talk to Bryan about everything I had found and noticed, especially the liquor bottles. The reaction I got from my husband nearly floored me. The same husband who was in the passenger seat napping beside me while I drove for those 21 hours. I'll never forget his exact words.

He said, "You bitch! You marked the bottles? What the hell did you do that for?"

I went upstairs to our bedroom and slammed the door. About 30 minutes went by before David came upstairs, crying.

"I'm sorry," he said. "You were right. You know him better than I do. He just told me that everything you said was true. I'm so sorry. We'll do it your way from now on. I'm so sorry."

Finally. I really thought the tide had turned. I calculated the time I had left with Bryan and I hoped it wasn't too late for me to make a difference. He was usually good with me when David or Bucky weren't around to interfere.

I firmly believe kids need discipline and structure and feel safer when they have it. Bryan responded to it, just not when he knew he could play one of his parents to find a way out. But despite how honest we were with him about what his mother and siblings turned out to be, he was on the same path and we couldn't stop him. David and I didn't understand. Here were three examples of people who were *not* sober, *not* smart and *not* ambitious. It looked pretty bad to us and we thought Bryan had the same opinion, considering he often talked about going to college and getting away from them. What were we missing?

Later that spring, David flew to Florida by himself to get in a little golf and get to know the new neighbors. I was still teaching, but he was retired. I felt I could handle a couple of weeks at home with Bryan. David was gone just three days when I called him and told him I was shortening his vacation and he was coming home the very next day. Bryan was past the point of listening to me. I was angry, disappointed and surprised. The rebellious pothead was already a combination of Bucky, Cindy and Jack and I didn't want to deal with him. I resented the fact that I was not allowed to do any parenting years ago when I felt I could have made a difference. I wanted David back NOW. He created the monster. He should have to reign him in.

In retrospect, I wonder what would have happened if I didn't call David. I couldn't have made Bryan any worse by myself.

I was hoping that, once David got home, he'd finally turn into that authority father figure that Bryan needed. Since he was forced to cut his golf vacation short, I thought he'd be mad as hell and that would work in my favor. Instead he just acted as a buffer between Bryan and me, and Bryan slipped further away from both of us.

23

Wanted by the F.B.I.

Bryan's senior year of high school was almost uneventful except for that F.B.I. arrest and the television news crews parked on our front lawn. I guess I'd better elaborate.

I was already home from school, waiting for David who had promised to stop by the grocery store for something to put together for dinner. Waiting. Waiting. Waiting. Waiting until after 7 p.m. when I heard the car pull in the driveway. The front door opened and Bryan and David came in. Bryan headed straight upstairs to his room. I had not seen my husband so upset since that early morning pick up at the Newtown police station after his co-worker's wedding. What the hell did this kid do now?

David: Bryan got arrested.

Kerry: For what?

David: He and Tommy got arrested because some girl overheard them talking about doing something violent at school. She reported them.

This was several years after the student killings at Columbine High School in Colorado, and schools were still being hyper-vigilant about students who showed signs of possible violence.

Kerry: And?

David: They were only talking about a video game and she thought they were talking about doing something at school themselves. She's a freshman. She doesn't even know Bryan.

So already David is willing to blame someone other than Bryan for this episode.

Kerry: And you've been at school until now? It's 7 p.m.

David: No, at the police station. They had him in jail because the F.B.I. got called in.

Just when I thought I couldn't be surprised by anything these kids would do, Bryan did it. I never would have suspected he'd be the one pulled in by the F.B.I. The only way I can describe this night is surreal. It was an out-of-body experience. I was stunned. Once I started thinking straight, I still couldn't comprehend a real honest-to-God F.B.I. arrest, and putting a 17-year-old in jail for a whole day instead of calling his parents into school when the incident happened. This was our Bryan! Granted, he had turned into a rebellious, lazy, spoiled brat, but I never saw signs of violence. (Later I found out it's because I hadn't looked.)

I was in for another night of watching my husband cry about the children he refused to discipline. You reap what you sow. When are you going to get it? This had the potential to be the biggest "I told you so" of all times. If I was lucky, it could be the rock bottom David needed to hit in order to climb out of the pit of clueless parenting. If I was lucky.

There was so much to think about. The ol' *Hr* name was going to hit the newspapers again. Oh but wait, that wouldn't happen until tomorrow. Tonight, the television news crews were setting up for live shots on our front lawn. We were the top story *and* the tease between the prime time shows that evening. I didn't even have time to call *my* school principal to warn him about the publicity.

Bryan claimed he told the truth from the moment the principal called him into the office. He said he and Tommy were only talking about video games and the eavesdropping little freshman girl blew it all out of proportion. But since it was a potentially violent situation, the principal said he was obligated to report it to the local police. Their protocol, since Columbine, was to call in the F.B.I. for school violence, even though there were no weapons involved and the two boys were doing all this talking *in class*, not out hiding behind the dumpsters or in a bathroom stall. Talk about making a mountain out of a mole hill!

It took a couple of hours, but Bryan and David recovered their composure enough to do a t.v. interview to tell Bryan's side of the story. They did a good job too. I think anybody who saw it probably sympathized with David as the parent of a typical teenage boy who got caught up in a big mess just because of those kids with the guns at Columbine. I felt better after we watched the segment on the 11 o'clock news.

I also felt better after confronting the principal at Bryan's school. He said he called us when the problem occurred that morning. He lied. We were still spending $8.25 per month for that caller ID at home and we both had cell phones. The school had all three numbers on Bryan's emergency contact list. They also had my number at work and Bucky's number too. None of us got a phone call while Bryan was sitting in a cell all afternoon. The principal admitted to me that Bryan had never been in trouble at school before and he was reluctant to believe Bryan could be involved in any violent act. But he didn't speak about Tommy. That was likely the key as to why Bryan and Tommy were locked up. The principal wanted to get rid of Tommy. We didn't know that until their court appearance. Tommy was a whole peck of trouble, in and out of school. Bryan was his latest recruit.

David relied on me for guidance during this entire episode. I think he was emotionally exhausted. He wanted my approval for going on the news. He wanted me to confront the principal, supposedly because I was a teacher and we spoke the same language. And although he didn't say it, I know he wanted me to comfort Bryan and convince him that nobody would believe something so outlandish about him. The only thing he didn't ask for was help with the F.B.I.

In the few moments I had to myself on that notorious night, my mind wandered. Of course, I thought about the crown. I was going to set a new level in this friendly competition. Even I never thought the bar would go this high. This one episode would keep me in the lead for quite a while.

I thought about the thousands of news shows Julie and I had done as reporters. But to have one of our stepkids featured as a criminal in the tease between prime time shows, well, that was new territory.

And I thought about the F.B.I. I knew Kevin's girls never got arrested by the F.B.I. The J.-Edgar-Hoover-Efrem-Zimbalist-Jr.-F.-freakin'-B.-I. What a night!

The only real contact I ever had with the F.B.I. was at Ruth's Chris Steakhouse in Jackson, Mississippi. I was a friend of the manager, Tico Hoffman, and was often around when his cronies were drinking and dining late into the night after closing. One of those cronies was Cletus, the local F.B.I. agent. I remember thinking he must have been excellent at undercover work because he reminded me of a cross between Wally Cox and Barney Fife. He was small, bespectacled and kind of cute in a nerdy sort of way. But it's not like I was going to call on Cletus for help in Connecticut, so I never even bothered to tell David about my F.B.I. connection. If he ever finds out, he's likely to yell at me for not doing all I could to help Bryan. Yep, that's *exactly* what he would do. I'll be taking that Cletus connection to my grave.

24

It's Been a Long Day Emails

Dear Julie,

How was your day?

I'm dead tired from all the excitement around here. Of course I put in a full day of teaching, but that was nothing compared to what happened at home.

After school, I was supposed to cook dinner, but David didn't get home until after 7 and somehow neglected to stop at the grocery store like he promised me this morning. His excuse this time was that he was delayed by the F.B.I. David had to pick up Bryan from jail. The F.B.I. removed him and his friend Tommy from school this morning and held them all day. They finally called David late in the afternoon. When they got home, they were accosted by several television news crews on our front lawn. They eventually did an interview with my former station.

I'll call you tomorrow with the details. Just wanted to let you know that now I'm 3-for-3 also. I thought I could save this one. I really did. Silly me.

Kerry

Hey Ker,

Sorry for your tough day. Call anytime. I'll be polishing the crown for you. But really, we're just tied again. And you couldn't save him. You and I have no power with these kids. We never did and we never will. That's the really sad part. All we can do is watch.

Julie

25

Choices at Starbucks

There are so many choices you have to make when you walk into a Starbucks. Tall, grande, venti, latte, cappucino, espresso, full roast, blonde roast, special roast, green tea, chai tea, iced tea, iced chai tea latte, 2%, skim, half 'n' half, caramel, mocha, frappucino, and I think I've made my point. That's what's wrong with the business model for that place. Well, that and the high prices. In fact, faced with the choice of Dunkin' Donuts or Starbucks, if they were next door to each other, I think most people would choose DD just so they wouldn't have to make more than one goddamned choice.

But for a lesson on choices, Starbucks was the perfect place to take Bryan. I had made a choice to dump him in favor of David.

I picked up Bryan after school and told him we were making a pit stop at Starbucks before we went home. When we got there, we both took several minutes to decide what we wanted to drink. Then I chose a table and he knew he was in for a *talk*.

Bryan and I communicated well, until his violent alcoholic episodes began during college. We had respect for each other too. As a high school teacher, I was more prepared for the rebellious antics of his teenage years than David. I just figured we'd punish him, he'd suffer and survive, and then we'd all move past it. That worked when I was growing up. I've seen it work with my girlfriends' kids. But in my home with David and Bryan, it was the absence of parent-imposed consequences that created the problems. It hurt me to watch Bryan growing out of control because he never learned the value of discipline, self-discipline, integrity and responsibility. Or if he did, he dismissed it because he had role models who were selfish and only blamed others for their problems. His mother was a master and his sister was on her way to topping Bucky in the blame game. Pizza Boy didn't play it straight either, and Bryan saw all of them survive on Daddy Welfare. He knew he could count on that too. And he didn't have to do a damn thing to get it. In fact, the less he did, the more welfare he could count on.

Although David consulted me about everything that had to do with Bryan, he rarely took my advice. I don't know why he even bothered asking me. Maybe he just hoped for approval. And I couldn't give it honestly. I never understood, and still don't, how a parent can keep indulging a child regardless of the outcome. The outcomes were never good. Why keep doing the same thing?

After their divorce, it appears that neither David nor Bucky took custody of the parenting handbook. I was the one who insisted on attending Parents' Night at school and other activities. I was the one who got to know the other parents in the neighborhood. I was the one who asked about homework and projects and grades. Remember, his mother placed no importance on grades and his father was already rattled from the misadventures of the two older kids. I felt like I was the only one in Bryan's corner and, until I got worn down and thought about my own marriage going down the drain, I probably was the only one thinking about his future. I wanted him to become self-sufficient and independent of his screwed-up family. If he didn't get away from them, I knew they'd drag him down.

Bryan's interests were amazingly similar to mine. That's what made me confident in taking on the role of stepmother when he came to live with us. He was searching for a mentor and a friend and I tried to be one. During my teaching years, he saw me shooting and editing video with my students after school and on weekends. He wanted to learn too, so I taught him and he got pretty good at it. I was also the one who taught him how to drive.

When we talked about what he'd like to be when he grew up, his top choice was always a teacher or a writer. Hey, that's me too. Guess I had some influence. Looking back, I might have lost it all on this very afternoon at Starbucks. I was beat. I couldn't take another day of fighting with my husband about his children and their behavior. It was clearly a parenting problem and neither parent was willing to admit that. They were willing to blame each other though. And after putting up with two non-educated and non-productive adult children, their third child was about to be set on the same path. Hell, he already had an F.B.I. arrest.

When we sat down at Starbucks, I told Bryan I wanted to tell him about some choices I had made that were going to affect him. The way things were going at home after the F.B.I. fiasco, he probably thought his dad was in for divorce number two. I assured him that was not going to happen. In fact, it was just the opposite.

On this afternoon at Starbucks, I was quitting my stepmothering job in order to save my marriage and that's exactly what I told Bryan. I told him I was tired of arguing with my husband about his lack of parenting skills. It took too much time and energy and it didn't do any good. I was exhausted.

I said, "Your father is now in charge of you. I'm not going to be involved in your schooling anymore, or in what I think should be done about chores and discipline at home. It only creates problems for your father and me and I'm not willing to argue anymore. Considering the way your brother and sister turned out, I'm sure you know your parents aren't the smartest ones in the PTA, but he's your father and I'm not your mother. I'm saving my marriage instead of saving you. I'm sorry, but that's how it's going to be from now on."

I don't remember what Bryan said, but I do remember the look on his face when I told him I was getting out of his life. Strangely, it wasn't relief. It was a look that said, "Oh boy, what now?" I seriously think he was worried about the total lack of control in his future. Except for me, no one tried to hold him accountable or question his actions. And up to this point, he wasn't doing well even under the little bit of control I had from time to time.

I also explained to him that I knew he needed saving, or at least guidance. But my best efforts were not respected and it was time to stop banging my head against the same brick wall. I had been trying to help David with Bryan since he was five years old, when both his parents allowed him to stay up late and watch the adult cartoon, *South Park*, on television. I was appalled at their ignorance and told them so, but nothing changed. He was now 17. It took me those 12 years in between to come to the conclusion that neither of his parents would ever see the value of discipline, consequences or rules. As a teacher, it killed me to let go. I felt like I was leaving the scene of an accident. It wasn't the right thing to do for Bryan, but I needed to look away and move on.

David just assumed his children would turn out like him – responsible and conservative. Instead, they turned out just like their mother – irresponsible and manipulative. She seemed okay with that. David was greatly disappointed but didn't take any action to try and turn things around. I had hoped I could save Bryan from following in the footsteps of Pizza Boy and Drunk Girl, but I couldn't.

It wasn't easy for me to follow through with my hands-off promise. It took a while for Bryan and David to get used to it too.

Bryan would still ask me for permission to do things. My new response was, "Go ask your father please."

As usual, David kept asking me about everything concerning Bryan. I'd answer, "I'm sure whatever you decide will be just fine, dear. You're his father." And David would get mad at me for that too. I couldn't win. He said I didn't care anymore. I told him I did care, just not so much.

I guess no one was happy with this arrangement. But it did cut down on the arguing. I took that as a sign of validation for my decision. David and I had no kids together. There was no reason for us to parent together, right? Except for one thing: I was the only one who had been acting as a parent.

So maybe I made the wrong choice that day at Starbucks.

26

Cats & Kids

For as long as David and I have been together, I have had two cats. I started with one long ago and then realized they're better in pairs, just like people. As they grow old and die, I always get another to be a friend for the one that remains. There are times when the first week or so is a challenge, but they always buddy up sooner or later.

David is a dog person. We have those too, usually just one at a time, except for the time when we had to take in Pizza Boy's dog because, well, you know. I guess dog people are used to putting a bowl of food down and watching it get devoured in seconds. We cat people are different. We put the bowl down in the same place, at the same time every day, but we never expect it to be woofed down in seconds. Cats are finicky. You've seen the t.v. commercials.

David doesn't get it. He opens the can of Fancy Feast, spoons it into two little bowls and then puts one down in front of each cat. Really, *in front of each cat* no matter where they are. On the couch, on our bed, on the dining room table, on the windowsill, on the kitchen counter. As you might imagine, several of those places are "NO-cat zones" when I catch them. They're smart enough to know not to get on the kitchen counter or dining room table when mom is around. But

David doesn't care. He just expects them to eat when and where he feeds them. If they don't eat when he puts the bowl in front of them, he follows them around with it for quite a while. It's amusing to watch, even though I know it will encourage some bad kitty habits.

Eventually he says to me, "Something's wrong with the cats. They're not eating."

I say, "They're cats. They'll eat when they're hungry."

Over the years I've tripped over bowls in the strangest places. Now that I think about it, maybe it's amusing from a cat's perspective too. Maybe they're just doing it to screw with him. Nah. They're cats.

Catering to the cats is the same way David treated his boys when they used to visit us in Florida. He'd constantly ask them if they wanted anything to eat or drink. He'd deliver it to them wherever they were. They didn't have to move a muscle. This was also amusing to watch, considering I had never seen him be the chief cook and bottle washer at any other time in our relationship. He'd make sandwiches, salads, ice tea, coffee, anything they wanted and put it right in front of their noses. I'm surprised he didn't follow them outside and light their cigarettes. Remember, these *boys* were over 21 and they should have been capable of feeding themselves. They hadn't starved at home up until now. But when they were at our house, David somehow felt the need to do everything for them. And they let him. Actually, it was disgusting to watch.

I remember the first time I pointed out to David that he treated our cats like his kids and it was wrong for all of them. Give a man a fish and you feed him for a day. Teach a man to fish and he'll feed himself for a lifetime. If the cats were hungry, they had to learn to get off their furry little asses and get over to their dishes and eat. If the boys wanted something, they should have to get off their asses too, right? There comes a time when daddy has to stop providing for grown men. As usual, he said my analogy was stupid. I'll bet the cats understand.

David has always said he wants to leave his children *something*. Unfortunately, his *something* is money. That's the problem. *Something* is *always* money in David's world and that's what his children were brought up to believe. If you got something from dad, it was money or something that cost money. They never had to do anything for money. Ever. No work involved. No chores. Not even demands for good grades at school because their mother said it was "enough just to be good people." And we all know how that turned out. Their father has only been a bank to them because that's what they learned from watching their mother. Everything was about money. Money for new clothes. Money for new furniture. Money for a bigger house. Money for toys. Money for vacations. Money for Christmas presents. He made it and Bucky spent it. She taught the kids to want it. After the divorce, she taught the kids various ways, some illegal, of how to get it, leading by example.

In reality, I know we all got money from our parents. The thing is, that wasn't all we got. I gained the knowledge that if I wanted money, I had to do something for it. When I was little, I remember getting a dollar or two for a good report card. But as the years went on, that stopped because I somehow learned that school was my job and I needed to do well to earn scholarships for college. There it is: the work ethic. Words like *job* and *earn* were clearly in my vocabulary at an early age. I must have learned them somewhere. Maybe it helps that I grew up in New England with immigrant grandparents and blue collar parents. David did too. I learned that hard work pays off, and not only in cash. It gave me a sense of pride, sometimes public accolades, and often the feeling of a job well done, a restful feeling. It's not all about money. There's so much more to life. That's a foreign concept to the gruesome threesome.

They weren't taught how to work and earn. Think about it. That's a pretty big deal. Imagine if you didn't understand the concept of working for a living. What would you do? How would you live? David's kids ask daddy for money. They feel entitled to it.

They also weren't taught to do anything for the sake of pride or a sense of accomplishment. This one is a little difficult for me to understand, considering they were surrounded by others who had achievements. Classmates, cousins, their father. Everyone around them was doing something. Why weren't they? They weren't living in a negative environment. They were encouraged and supported like any other kids. They just seemed to have an attitude of superiority, like they knew they didn't have to do anything specific, yet they could do what they wanted. Where did this come from? In my world, parents are supposed to put some kind of demands on their kids. How do you learn to be responsible if you aren't given responsibility for something? How can you learn self-discipline if you don't get disciplined?

Jack actually played high school football. There's an opportunity for discipline. Unfortunately, he had to stop when he hurt his knee. And then the whole high school thing went down the drain when he didn't graduate because of that so-called incompetent guidance counselor. Nothing to be proud of there. And as I've said before (over and over), the only job he's ever had is delivering pizzas. There's not a lot of applause, awards or promotions in that world. I mean, could you even describe the last pizza delivery guy who came to your door? It's a cash-only transaction.

Cindy was in the drama club in high school. I saw her in one play and she basically played herself. The character was moody and had tantrums. She did a very good job and everybody told her so, me included. She went on to one semester of drama school after high school, but that was it. She didn't have the discipline.

Bryan played a couple of musical instruments and tried baseball and track along the way in school. He just didn't stick with anything long enough to get good at it. He didn't seem to like the whole idea of practicing to get better. Watching his mother, brother and sister drinking and smoking and hanging around was just too tempting a lifestyle for him. He got sucked in. And why not? There were no expectations or demands and he still got money from dad. Daddy Welfare instead of an allowance.

Think about some of the kids you grew up with who didn't excel at anything. Chances are, some of them are engineers now. How about the class clown? He might be headlining in Vegas. The fat kid who never got selected for kickball probably became a slim personal trainer, or at least slim. We turn things around. Some of our weaknesses turn out to be our greatest strengths when we are left to our own resources. I've been told I was a very shy child, yet I grew up to work on television.

We all grow up to have some element of success in our lives regardless of our childhood. Whether it's a career, a family, a skill, a talent or a larger mission, we grow up to do *something*. Not everyone is dependent on their daddy or welfare, or Daddy Welfare, into their 30s and 40s.

Remember potty training? Somewhere along the line you learned to wipe your own ass and take pride in the accomplishment. You discovered how to whip up some mac and cheese if you wanted to eat. And you loved it the first time someone called you a "big girl."

Most of us don't have someone putting a bowl of food down in front of us. That's a good thing. It pushes you up the learning curve. It's what separates the men from the cats! And I'll be damned if I'm going to let my husband turn my cats into fucking pizza boys!

27

Kids & Cats

After Bryan's F.B.I. arrest with his friend Tommy in his senior year of high school, David finally came to the conclusion he should enforce some form of restriction on the kid. After all, by this time he realized the other two would not be setting the world on fire (well, maybe literally, but not figuratively). Now it was time to put Bryan on the straight and narrow. It was David's first solo attempt at punishment and he was flying by the seat of his pants. He decided that Bryan could no longer pal around with Tommy and he also had to be home before dark.

As for hanging out with Tommy, David couldn't keep them apart at school. And they got arrested in the morning. It had nothing to do with darkness. David had quite a bit to learn about the punishment fitting the crime. He also had a lot to learn about sticking to the punishment you dish out, whatever it is.

Tommy wasn't a bad-looking kid. I mean, you couldn't tell he was a juvenile delinquent just by looking at him. He was pleasant enough to your face. But if I go on, I'll just be describing Eddie Haskell from *Leave It to Beaver*. You get the idea. What you see is not exactly what you get.

David was working but I took the day off to accompany Bryan to court for that arrest. Perhaps it should have been the other way around, ya think?

I just about got the wind knocked out of me when the prosecutor said to the judge, "Your honor, I really don't know what to say about this boy Thomas. In all my years as a prosecutor, I've never seen such a long record of offenses for such a young person."

Yep, Bryan sure can pick 'em. Now I see this as an early sign of Bryan's co-dependency. He needed to be with someone like Tommy so that he would look good in comparison. Heck, *Rosemary's Baby* would look good in comparison to Tommy.

When we got home I told David all about the prosecutor's take on Tommy. He looked surprised. Not deer-in-the-headlights surprised, but moderately taken aback. He didn't appear to be as worried about their friendship as I was. I think he had faith that Bryan was a good kid. Blind faith. I, on the other hand, knew Bryan was a follower and feared what would happen next if he and Tommy stayed together.

It was less than a couple of weeks later that I discovered David's idea of punishment was just that: an idea. It was seriously lacking in the follow-through department. Ever since court, Bryan continued to be home before dark and we didn't see Tommy or hear his name. But like I said, it was *less than two weeks later* and that was over.

I came home from school at about 4 p.m. and had to wait to pull in the driveway because someone was backing out. Yikes! It was Tommy's car and he and Bryan were in it. They took off and I parked and sat in the driveway, thinking about how I should calmly tell David that the boys were back together and probably up to no good. Bryan was defying his father's new rules. His father's first-ever rules. I secretly hoped this would crush David. This slap in the face would no doubt make him take his fatherhood gig a little more seriously. I mean really, it wasn't just an arrest. It was a freakin' F.B.I. arrest, complete with television news reporters parked on our front lawn for live shots!

When I went into the house, David was watching t.v. in the family room.

I calmly said, "I just saw Tommy pull out of the driveway with Bryan in the car."

"I know," he said.

"You know? Why did you let him go out with Tommy?" I asked, still calm.

I wish I was sitting down for his answer. I couldn't believe it. Neither will you.

David said, and I'm not even kidding, "He asked me."

"He asked you? He asked you?" I yelled. The calm had left me. "What do you mean, he asked you? Just because he asked you doesn't mean you should let him. Don't you remember what we just went through? Can't you ever use the word *no*?"

Now he looked deer-in-the-headlights surprised.

"What do you mean?" he asked. "He was *honest* with me and asked me if he could go out with Tommy. He promised they'll be home before dark."

As many of us have told our parents, there's nothing you can do in the dark that you can't do in the daylight. And was he brain dead? Drunk? On drugs? My husband, I mean. Not Bryan. How could David let Bryan go off with Tommy less than two weeks after we found out about Tommy's long arrest record? And as for the honesty, well, I don't know where that little ploy came from, but I've got to hand it to Bryan. It worked. I guess it didn't matter what he was going to do or whom he was going to do it with as long as he was *honest* about it. Worked for David. Not for me.

Kids don't know what's good for them. Like one of my favorite rock 'n' roll philosophers says, "You can't always get what you want."

But kids don't know that and they keep trying. Kids need someone to say "no" because they lack the experience to use that word themselves.

"No! Because I said so."

"No, because I'm the mommy!"

Or just plain "No!" That one word is a very powerful complete sentence if you use it as such.

Kids need guidance in order to stay safe and healthy as they grow. That's what parents are for: to show them the way and slap them upside the head when they need to make an adjustment.

Whether it's food, friends, life's lessons, whatever. Let a teenage boy decide what to do for himself and he'd eat pizza and donuts all day while spending time with the top-heavy hooker at the motel on the hill and then skateboard down the motel driveway into four lanes of traffic. Yeah, I know I'm exaggerating here, but probably not by much. My point is, kids are generally stupid about many things. And stupid hurts. Luckily, stupid is just part of life and most learn some lessons and grow out of it. They should at least grow out of it by the time they are parents for God's sake! Even the so-called parents of cats.

<u>Five years later, 7 a.m.</u>

Today I had to get up early for my favorite 90-minute yoga class. Serenity now! I need that.

The first thing I do is feed the animals. Cats first, dog next. Zeke Cat is always the first one ready to eat. He waits at his place mat while I fix the dishes on the kitchen counter. Eddie Cat is not far behind, but he never beats Zeke to breakfast. Well this morning, Eddie was waiting and I couldn't find Zeke. I kept calling his name as I went from room to room. I even shook the container of kitty treats because that sound always brings both of them running. But still no Zeke.

So I went to our bedroom and said to my sleeping husband, "David, I can't find Zeke."

David bolted upright and said, "I forgot! He's in the garage."

Yes he was. The poor thing was in the garage all night long and he was waiting at the door. His daddy had forgotten him.

Zeke is the adventurous type. The woman we got him from used to walk him outside on a leash. But since we have a big, screened-in patio out back, I figure that's enough *outside* for him now. There's plenty of room to run around, lots of furniture to jump on and a dozen plants to explore. However, Zeke will still try to get on the other side of a closed door to the outside world. He sits at the front door, the door to the garage, and the patio door to the backyard, just waiting for one of them to open so he can dart out and go on a little adventure. He doesn't go far and he doesn't run away. He just likes to go out.

On the previous night, I had already gone to bed and David was up watching t.v. He was being the dutiful, or so he thought, daddy in letting the little boy out in the garage to have some fun.

He explained, "Zeke was throwing himself against the door to the garage. I've never seen him do that. He really wanted to go out, so I let him in the garage for awhile."

In other words, *Zeke asked him if he could go out and play in the garage.* Hey, he was an *honest* little kitty. What else could David do?

And by the way, I don't really think Zeke "threw himself against the door." Even if he did, that was no reason for David to let him out. The garage is no place for a kitty, especially when David's "awhile" turned out to be all night because he forgot about the little guy. Use some grown-up parental judgment please. Try out that "no" word, even if it's just on the cat.

It's the Bryan and Tommy scene all over again.

Zeke wanted out and David let him out, despite what the outcome could be. Now I love Zeke, but Zeke's a cat and there are tons of things in our garage that cats should not be around. They don't know this because they're cats. There are dirty, greasy things, fertilizers and pesticides, glass bottles that could be knocked off shelves, perhaps a few bugs in the corners, you know, *things*. Our next-door neighbors once had a small alligator in their garage and we're four houses away from the nearest lake! Our garage is not childproof, cat-proof or gator-proof.

I'll admit the emotional mom in me always feels a tiny bit sorry for Zeke when I see him pining away at the door. But the mom with a brain knows he's better off when I confine his exploration to a large house and screened-in patio complete with kitty toys, kitty condos and kitty scratching posts. In this case, mother knows best.

What does father know? Father knows shit. In fact, David knew shit firsthand on this morning because Zeke didn't hold it overnight and I was not about to clean up a mess that would have been correctly deposited in the pine-pellet-filled litter box if his daddy hadn't let the little critter have his own way. *"He asked me."* So David got out of bed at 7:30 a.m. to clean the kitty shit off the floor of the garage.

Cats and children do not instinctively know what's good for them. Leave a cat out in the wild and well, you know, the circle of life. Leave a kid out in the wild and well, the circle of life looks like a good outcome from where I'm sitting. No shit.

28

Ah, to have a Son in College

A fter producing two kids who were welfare cases and who seemed to have no drive or potential to do anything other than drink and smoke, you'd think Bucky would have somehow been supportive of the one kid who made it to college. No such luck.

We moved to Florida right after Bryan got out of high school. We hoped he would come with us and go to the University of Florida, and stay far away from his mother and siblings. On one of our trips to Florida before the move, he and I took the three-hour drive from Orlando to the home of the Florida Gators and did the campus tour. I loved it. But he wanted to stay in Connecticut and go to UCONN. However, he didn't want to spend summers and holidays with his mother and sister. His brother was living in an apartment with a roommate at the time. So the summer after his senior year of high school, Bryan chose to live with his friend Nate and his family in our old neighborhood. Nate's parents didn't seem to mind. Bucky didn't seem to mind. She didn't have to deal with him or feed him. And honestly by that time, he was so much like his older siblings and his mother that we couldn't wait to fly south. He was over 18 and making his own choices. We were providing him with a college education. We hoped for the best.

Bryan had once told me that Nate's parents were drinkers. But every time I saw them and talked to them, they seemed sober. They had jobs. However, their sons didn't. They had an older son who was still living at home and not doing anything with his life and Nate had no plans for college. So it was the same smoking and drinking environment that Bryan had at his mom's. Once again, we hoped for the best.

That first year at UCONN, Bryan's mother somehow managed to get him to and from school for a couple of holidays, and we thought things would be fine. After all, it's not like she had to drive him to class, just pick him up for Thanksgiving, Christmas and spring break. Less than two hours on the road, that's all. Little did we know, his roommate's mother was actually providing the transportation.

Bryan's roommate, Bill, lived near Bucky. In fact, Bill's mom and Bucky used to be friends. But in this first year of college, Bill's mom got an inside look at how Bucky both used, and neglected Bryan, and she broke off the friendship. She started to make excuses for why Bryan could not get a ride to and from school with her and her son. The car was always too full or they were going at an inconvenient time. She wanted nothing to do with her old pal or Bryan. Maybe she was trying to send Bucky a message that she should take some responsibility for her own son. Bill's mom didn't realize that a lesson like that always fell on deaf ears with Bucky.

I wish we paid more attention to what Bill's mom was doing and why. That might have been the big clue we missed early on that would have enlightened us about Bryan's problems with alcohol. Most mothers, seeing Bryan's need for rides to and from school, probably would have helped. Was Bill's mom really trying to teach Bucky a lesson or did she want to keep her son away from Bryan as much as possible. Did she already know he was a bad influence? After all, Bill lived with him. He must have said something to his mom about Bryan. What did Bill's mom know and when did she know it? We wish she would have shared it with us.

In his sophomore year, Bryan was left to try to find rides home and the phone calls began. Bucky didn't want to make the one-hour drive to pick him up for Christmas break. What kind of mother doesn't want her son home for Christmas? What did she expect us to do, drive up from Florida? She called us with some lame excuse about her car not being good enough to make the trip. Hardly. The loan company mistakenly called us several times regarding the payments being late. It was practically new. She also said Pizza Boy Jack's car wasn't good enough to make the trip. Well, that was true. We bought him several used cars and he always seemed to run them into the ground despite the fact that their previous owners kept them up perfectly. One used car was from my Uncle Pete, who was the proverbial little old man who only drove to church on Sundays and followed the maintenance schedule in the book to the letter. That tank of an Oldsmobile lasted for less than a year with Pizza Boy.

Bucky's solution was to ask David to pay for a rental car so she could go and get him. Really. Honest to God I am not kidding. With a car sitting in front of her apartment, she wanted her ex-husband to rent her another car so she could drive an hour to pick up her son (the one she had sold for $25,000) and drop him off at Nate's house because she also had no room for him at her apartment. Come on now, even if you don't have a guest room, you make room for family. After all, this was her only kid who made it to college. She couldn't even celebrate his efforts on his school breaks by at least putting a roof over his head. The Mother of the Year Prize Patrol couldn't speed by this one fast enough.

Bryan ended up getting a ride to Nate's house with another student who lived in the area.

Bucky didn't mind if Bryan used her address when he wanted to do some banking though. The kid was living in his father's Land of Denial for his first year of college, thinking his mother would help him when he needed it. So instead of doing his own banking with the checks from his college work-study job, he sent them to her to deposit. She deposited them all right. She deposited them into her own account which was probably directly linked to the local convenience store for her cigarette and wine tab. She actually stole his first few checks which totaled a little less than $400. Can you imagine? And that's really the end of her story. No apology to Bryan. She told him to get money from his father. So that's where he turned, again and again and again. But he was learning. The expensive college education taught him nothing in those first couple of years compared to all that he learned about his mother.

When it came time to go back to school after that second Christmas, we were waiting to see who would take him. Bucky said she wouldn't do it. Jack claimed his car wouldn't make it. Bill's mom honestly said she wouldn't do it because it was his mother's responsibility. So Bryan called us with his dilemma. And from 1,300 miles away, David started scrambling for a driver. Cousin Emma was not a good choice. After all she was now calling Bryan a liar and Pizza Boy much worse. Besides, I called her to warn her to have an excuse ready. She did. David then tried his old friend Frank, who was able to come up with an excuse on his own. Over the years, Frank was well aware of what Jack had turned out to be and probably was anticipating the same for Bryan. Also, David only called him when he wanted something, usually a job for one of the kids who couldn't get one on his own. Poor Frank, a carpenter, suffered with Jack briefly before he just came out and said the kid was too lazy to do anything.

Now Cindy could have taken her mother's car to drive him. I'm not sure why that didn't happen. She'd had some accidents which might have been attributed to drinking, so maybe Bryan didn't ask her or maybe she was in a drunk tank somewhere and just wasn't around. That was the Christmas David got a letter from her, rather than a phone call, asking for money. So we really didn't have much contact with her then and that was nice.

So who would take Bryan to school? Greyhound. Sure, every college has bus service. However, when you miss a connection.... Bryan missed the connection. It was Bill who somehow managed to get him from the bus station back to the dorm. That was another clue we missed: Bill was the reliable one. I wish we noticed it then.

29

The Only College Graduation You'll Ever Attend

Bryan should have graduated from college in May of 2009. But he flunked out in 2008. That's the year he talked David into letting him move into an apartment off campus. Neither of us thought it was a good idea and I said "no" from day one. Bryan tried every excuse in the book for not going back to the dorm. It was too noisy to study, he had to share a bathroom and he had a shy bladder, too many distractions, whatever. David finally gave in. He said he was mostly concerned about Bryan's shy bladder and felt he would be better off with his own bathroom.

Now I could have reminded him of all the wonderful places we visited with Bryan over the years and all the times he used public bathrooms. The three of us went to Disney World, movie theaters, restaurants, all the Smithsonian buildings in Washington, D.C., Amtrak trains, airplanes, Yankee Stadium. He never had any problems peeing in any of those bathrooms during his first 20 years. Have you seen the bathrooms at major league ballparks? If you can pee there, you can pee anywhere. What was so different now? Yes, I could have reminded him, but I didn't. This was not a battle I picked.

In the first semester of 2008, Bryan painted us a picture of how wonderful college life was, especially now that he was in an apartment. David encouraged him to get his grades up because, supposedly, there were no distractions anymore. Over the past two years Bryan had dropped classes and gotten several low grades. So now David told him that his future at the apartment was riding on his ability to raise his grade point average. If not, he'd have to go back to the dorm. I think most kids would have risen to the challenge. Not Bryan. He had never experienced consequences, so he (correctly) never expected any.

By the end of the semester, the apartment dweller flunked everything and tried to buy time by telling his father it was because his roommate, Bill, was an alcoholic and Bryan couldn't be around him and concentrate enough to study. Everything that went wrong, from Bryan's grades to unpaid utility bills, was Bill's fault, according to Bryan. And honest to God, David said he believed him. He kept telling me the stories that Bryan was telling him. They were probably true, except the names were changed to protect the guilty one. It was Bryan who was the actual drunk and I'm sure Bill was having a hard time living with him. This caused a lot of tension between David and me. I know I said "I told you so" once in a while regarding the apartment situation. Of course, outwardly to David, I was only referring to Bryan's troubles because of his roommate. I wondered if David knew that Bryan was lying to him. He might have. He just didn't want to admit it because, if he did, he was going to be 0-for-3 on raising successful children.

A college graduate in the family was not on the horizon for David. But a college graduation was. Even if I had to drag him kicking and screaming.

Years earlier, I had connected with a needy family through a charity called The Box Project. Jeannette and her son Christopher lived in Tunica, Mississippi. They were African Americans. She had worked as a domestic for white families during her adult life until she became disabled due to obesity and the health problems that resulted from her weight. She never married. Her son went to a private Catholic school in Memphis, about an hour away from home. She told me that the white families she had worked for helped to get Christopher into the school. He was a bright boy. They wanted him to succeed and they obviously cared for Jeannette.

During the whole time Jeannette was employed, she was unable to buy a house because no one would give her a mortgage. But as soon as she became disabled, she qualified and bought a house in the white section of Tunica. Yes, she knew how ridiculous it was to finally get a house when she wasn't working. (Our screwed-up government programs at work.) She also knew that she and her son probably were not wanted in this neighborhood, but she was determined that Christopher would have a better life than the other black kids she saw being raised and schooled in Tunica.

Christopher excelled in school. He was in the choir and on the school newspaper staff. He also had a job at the local library. There was no doubt he would go to college and Jeannette was over the moon about that. Unfortunately, she would not live to see it. In his senior year of high school, Christopher lost his mother after a long series of illnesses. They were very close. It was always just the two of them and he was both her son and nursemaid during her last year.

There was no way Christopher could afford the house, and he moved on willingly because he was going to college at Jackson State University. He ended up spending his school vacations with his aunt and her family in Tunica, although he had few school vacations. He took as many classes as he could handle and that included summer school. He also took a work-study job at school so he could gain experience and references for his resume and his future. Jeannette taught him to plan ahead.

In May of 2009, I told David we were going to Christopher's college graduation. David had never met him and always dismissed any charity thing I had going on. He said he didn't want to go all the way to Mississippi just for a graduation and I should go by myself. I knew how much he would get out of meeting Christopher, so this was one of the battles I picked. All I said was, "You're going because it's the only college graduation you're ever going to attend. End of discussion!" And it was.

Christopher is the anti-Bryan, the anti-Cindy and the anti-Pizza Boy. In other words, except for the color of his skin, Christopher was the spitting image of David. He was a smart, hard worker who was about to make his own way in the world. And he accepted that responsibility, as did David so many years before. Christopher left college with an education that he was determined to use to become successful. That's what David did, without any help from parents paving the way with money, buying his way out of trouble.

We went to Jackson and stayed with Julie and Kevin for a few days. It was the first time David had met them in-person and he admired the way they lived with so many pets and with such a relaxed and casual way about them. We had a great time and enjoyed their hospitality.

Our tour of the Jackson area was highlighted by the trip to Jackson State on graduation day. It was like nothing David had ever seen before. First of all, it's a large university, much larger than the one David attended. And it was crowded, packed full of more African American people than David had ever seen in one place. It was familiar to me. The ceremony was in the gymnasium. As the only white female sportscaster in Jackson back in the '80s, I was often the easiest one to find in the crowd at the basketball games in that very gym. "Look, there's a white girl! Must be Kerry Kendall."

David had never been to Jackson, Mississippi or anywhere else in the Deep South. Although he grew up in a town that was practically next door to Bridgeport, Connecticut, I knew he really didn't experience the cultural mix that city had to offer. He was more comfortable staying in his own neighborhood. I attribute that to his generation as well as his upbringing. He was about to have a new experience as part of the white minority.

My witty friend Joyce gave me an interesting task on our trip. She told me to keep photographing David on the JSU campus, keeping the lens open wide to get him and all his surroundings. The pictures speak volumes. I know we weren't the only white people there that day, but it certainly felt that way to David. And it certainly looks that way in my photographs. Thanks Joyce. The photos bring back some great memories.

That evening, we took Christopher out to dinner and David finally got to talk to a successful, sober, college graduate who already had a full-time job and an apartment and a roommate. He got all of that *on his own*. He told us about his job and his plans to make money and *save* money. It was heartwarming to be at the same table with both of them. A boy who didn't have a father in his life and a father who didn't have a kid who would ever be as successful as Christopher felt at that very moment. He knew his mom would be proud. Heck, we were proud of him. It was a good feeling and I knew David was glad I dragged him to Jackson.

After that weekend I tried to engage David in conversation about what made Christopher so independent and self-sufficient, hoping he had learned something and would use it with his own children. But he didn't venture to guess, and dismissed any comparison with his kids. This is another one of those times I gave up the fight. Looking back, I wish I made him think about it more.

I'm sure Christopher did so well for himself because *he had to*. There was no place for him to go if he didn't stay on the right path toward graduation. He had no one to fall back on. His daddy wasn't standing by with a checkbook ready to buy him a do-over for his mistakes. He didn't have the luxury of flunking classes because, if he did, he'd lose his scholarship money. There was only one way out for him. He took it and made the most of it.

David's kids have never been put in that position. They can't learn from failure because they've always been bailed out, literally and figuratively. Some lessons are priceless. Others can't be bought, no matter how many times you try.

A couple of years after Christopher's graduation, Bryan went through yet *another* session of detox. When he got out and finally called his father, David told me Bryan sounded better than he had in a long time. That was logical. He hadn't been sober in a long time. He said Bryan told him he didn't want anything from him. He said he was going to get a job and support himself. He was staying with his mother and his alcoholic sister at the time. David was pleased and looked as if he really believed things would be getting better. After they hung up, he made the mistake of saying out loud that he wished Bryan would have gotten a job two years ago.

Bryan had spent the past two years living with his brother and taking one or two classes at a satellite branch of the college while David was paying the rent, car insurance and more for both of them. David justified this by saying he had to support Bryan while he was in school. Really? One or two classes is "in school" enough to get all living expenses? He also said he felt he had to help Jack because Jack was helping Bryan by letting him live at the apartment. Well, this was just too much for me. I'm only human and the teacher in me couldn't let this learning opportunity pass.

> Kerry: David, why do you think Bryan never got a job since he's been living with Jack?
>
> David: I don't know.
>
> Kerry: David, this is important for both you and Bryan. Just think about it for awhile. I'm not asking you for an answer now, but it's important that you know the answer to this question. Why hasn't Bryan gotten a job over the past two years?
>
> David: *(Getting mad at me for asking.)* I don't know! I guess he's lazy.
>
> Kerry: That's not the answer David. He may be lazy, but that's *not* why he hasn't gotten a job over the past two years. Please calm down and think. We'll talk later.

Less than five minutes went by and David couldn't stand it anymore.

David: Why? Why didn't Bryan get a job over the past two years?

Kerry: Because he didn't have to.

David: *(Walking away from me.)* You're right. Another hollow victory.

30

He Gets It, Sort Of

By the time David comes over to my side, the current crisis is over. He often tells me I was right and maybe he should have considered my advice. He's not stupid. I know he gets it. He says so. "I get it Kerry, now shut up." So I do, for the moment. But I try to find a way to repeat the lesson before he forgets it. He acknowledges that too, mostly with a glare.

He gets it from other people too. It's not just my advice to let the kids fend for themselves and hit rock bottom so they can begin the climb back up on their own. He's heard the same thing from psychologists, psychiatrists, doctors, nurses, people at Al-Anon meetings and very dear friends who have gone out of their way to share their own experiences and tell him that his methods are counter-productive to raising successful and independent children. So why does he think he's going to prevail with his way? Or does he?

He could be trying to buy his way out of guilt, but he doesn't have a lot to be guilty about. Bryan spent more time with David than anyone growing up. He never lacked time with his dad.

By the time he was divorced, David was cut out of Cindy's life because her mother started drinking and smoking with the young teenager. I'm sure Cindy also kept her distance because she felt guilty for accusing her father of molesting her. So that bond was broken by her mother, not by him. He did everything he could to try and maintain a relationship. Cindy was the one who said "no" to all invitations.

As for Jack, David wanted him to get good grades, not drink, not smoke pot and probably not make a career out of delivering pizzas. Jack didn't want to be lectured to by his dad, so he cut him off whenever David tried to help him plan a better future. Once again, David tried. I was there. I saw him try. And David's cousin Emma, whom David was living with after the divorce, also invited the kids over all the time. Yet we only saw Jack and Cindy at her house when they came by at Christmas to collect their gifts.

For someone like me, who didn't grow up with lots of money, these early years with David were eye-opening. I always thought that kids with money had it easy. Well, they do in some ways, but now I was seeing that having it easy is not necessarily a good thing.

How could someone like David, who has so much money to fix things, end up with three non-functioning dependents because of his money? I never believed my mom when she told me, "Money can't buy happiness." I do now. Parenting is hard work and work was always too easy for David. The just-throw-money-at-it method was failing him and he was unwilling to try anything else. He had money, but not happiness.

I know I must have a blind spot too. I think I've been a pretty good teacher. A lot of my students are very successful personally and professionally. Yet I haven't been able to get through to my own husband using concrete lessons from his own real-life experiences.

David keeps doing the same thing over and over and getting the same results. That's the definition of insanity, right? How do I teach him to let his children learn responsibility and self-discipline on their own, before more tragedy occurs? Why haven't I found the way? Why do I have to watch him fuel these same fires over and over again?

After the fact, I get, "You were right. I should have listened to you." So why doesn't he? And why hasn't Kevin ever listened to Julie?

Hell, if you're playing the odds at roulette, you'd think you'd bet on black once if you're always losing money on red. Why do these men think they know what they're doing when so many of their actions have failed?

And if man evolved from apes, why are there still apes?

These are just a few of the many questions that may never be answered in my lifetime. I'm okay with that as long as I have my coping skills (i.e. shopping, drinking, writing) and my dear friend Julie. Whenever one of us catches the other saying, "It could be worse," we just laugh out loud because we know it *has* been worse and it *will be* again. We'll drink to that.

31

Older Women are Smarter Women

I wish my dear friend Joan was still here. She always helped me to cope. Unfortunately she passed away from ovarian cancer in 2006, my 9th year of marriage. She started out as my high school English teacher but became a combination friend, mother and sage to all of the young women who were lucky enough to know her. She and her husband only had one son, so I guess she had a lot of *girl advice* stored up. Lunch among the teachers at school was like a therapy session when you needed it.

She once told a story of how her son John was trying to get his way by manipulating her and her husband in a way that put them on opposite sides. She nipped that in the bud by choosing her husband over her son. She was proud of it too. I couldn't believe it. A mother shouldn't do that, should she? As Joan explained, and as I learned first-hand many times in the years since, she should if she wants to stay happily married. Joan explained to the girls, just as she explained to her young son, that she intended to spend her life with Bill.

"John will grow up and get married, move away and have a family of his own," she said, "but Bill and I will be together until death do us part."

The lesson is to have a united front with your husband in matters concerning the kids, any kids. You will learn this so much sooner than your husband will, if he ever does.

During the first few years of our marriage while we were still living nearby David's children in Connecticut, they sometimes announced they were coming for a visit. Well, they never actually came just to see him. They usually came to get something *from* him and coincidentally had to see him in the process. I never wanted to be around for these heartwarming family gatherings, so I made excuses like I had to go shopping or visit a friend. David would see right through me and say, "You just don't want to see my kids." For a long time I did my best to lie my way out of it and insist that wasn't true. But that set up a confrontation which usually led to an argument about something, even if it wasn't about the kids. Confrontation eats away at marriage. Joan helped me eliminate the confrontation with her meatball-subs-for-Christmas-dinner story.

Joan and Bill hosted an annual Christmas party for family and friends. There was always a lovely buffet and you could count on the same good food every year because everyone brought what they did best. One of Joan's best was her meatballs and sauce. Every year (and by the time I heard this story from her, she and Bill had been married for over 30 years) she made her meatballs and sauce a few days before Christmas.

As Bill helped to get the house ready and made his shopping list for the last minute items he picked up on Christmas Eve, he always asked, "Joan, do you want me to pick up the sub rolls for the meatballs?"

And every year, without missing a beat, she answered, "No Bill, I already took care of that."

As Joan explained it to me, "Kerry, Bill thinks my answer means that I already got the sub rolls for the meatballs, so he doesn't have to. But what I actually mean is, there are no sub rolls to get because you've got to be crazy if you think I'm serving meatball subs for Christmas dinner."

No fuss, no fighting, no sarcasm, no mention of the past 30-plus years without sub rolls at Christmas dinner. Just answer the question, speak the truth, and move past it. It was like she dared me to be just as sly with my comebacks instead of sweating the small stuff.

From then on, when David's kids announced their visits while we were still living in Connecticut, I was ready. I'd tell David I was glad they were coming to visit him. What I actually meant was, I was glad they *weren't* coming to see me.

I'd have dinner ready to be heated, but I wouldn't be there. I didn't make an excuse, I just went out with a promise that I'd be home "later." And I was, much later.

When I got home, David would say something like, "You missed the kids again." I'd say, "I know. I hope you all had a good dinner." What I meant was, "Whew, I dodged another bullet and I hope they choked on dinner."

No confrontation and no lies. We both appeared to be on the same side. He couldn't fault me for not being prepared with dinner for our guests and I really did come home "later." Not another word was said and life went on.

A few years later, I pulled the same escape act in Florida when David invited both boys to come for a visit. I went to Sarasota to stay with my friend Joyce for a week.

David said, "The boys know you just don't want to be around when they're here." Joan was gone by then, so I had to channel her. I said, "That's okay. I'm sure they don't want to be around me either, so we all win." He couldn't argue with that.

Julie uses this method too. She loves the way it derails any chance of fighting.

Kevin's youngest daughter, Tracy, was about to get married for the fourth time. Julie used Joan's technique in having a quick discussion, and no argument, about a gift for the happy couple. But first, a little background is necessary.

This is the part of the book where you might think I'm exaggerating because the circumstances are incredibly outrageous. But honest-to-God, every word is true except for the name changes.

A fourth marriage was not unusual in Tracy's family circle. Both of her sisters had also been married three times. All but two of their collective children, seven of them, have different fathers and each of the fathers has custody of the kids. So these girls are just as undisciplined and irresponsible as David's brood.

Tracy had her one and only son before she left high school. She then married and divorced three husbands. After that, she moved in with her mother. During that time, she had an epiphany. She was marrying the wrong kind. She announced that she was a lesbian and moved in with her new lover. That relationship didn't last long and she was soon back with her mother. Then she had another epiphany. She wasn't a lesbian. So she went out hunting for husband number four. She found him and announced that there would be a "dressy-casual wedding" at his parents' house.

Julie wore a lovely ivory pantsuit and had Kevin wear gray slacks, a navy blue sports jacket, but no tie. That's her idea of dressy-casual and I concur. When they arrived, it appeared that the other guests only got the "casual" part of the invitation. The parents of the groom were in shorts and t-shirts. But Julie said the father's hair was neatly arranged in a nice long ponytail. Maybe that was his "dressy" part.

Back to the gift. Before they left for the wedding, Kevin asked Julie if she had done anything about a gift for Tracy.

Julie said, "Of course honey. I took care of it." Not another word was said.

Even if Kevin didn't have confidence that she'd get the perfect gift for her first stepdaughter's wedding, he had to be lulled into a sense of security by now. After all, practice makes perfect and Julie had plenty of practice. This was going to be the tenth gift for the tenth wedding among the three girls.

Julie's gift was a lovely bunch of flowers she picked up at the local Piggly Wiggly grocery store. She said they were pretty enough, and appropriate. The marriage wasn't likely to last, but at least it would probably outlast the life of their gift this time. That was something Tracy could brag about.

Kevin didn't even notice.

My friend Joan knew what she was talking about. You can be honest with your husband while avoiding confrontation. And with practice, Julie and I have learned you can even screw the kids in the process and get away with it.

As for Tracy's fourth marriage, it lasted about a year. Then she said she discovered that her husband was both a stalker and a pedophile. But hey, her marriage lasted longer than Julie and Kevin's gift. That's something.

32

Same Shit, Different Day Emails

Julie,

As you know, my dad is coming to stay with us for awhile. Now Bryan wants to come down too. Says he needs to get his life together. Ain't life grand?

Kerry

Ker,

Holy shit! You're a better woman than I am. You're going to have your dad and Bryan? My advice... buy a condo and you move into it. Let David, your dad and Bryan have the house!

Julie

Hey Ker,

Kevin's kids continue to be messed up. Not one is working right now. Terry is $480 late on her rent and keeps texting her dad that she doesn't know what she's going to do. Think I should tell her?

Julie

Julie,

Someone should tell her to get a fucking job. Might as well be you. Even if her father tells her, you'll get blamed for coming up with such a novel idea. And the other 2 queen bees?

Kerry

Ker,

The other 2 are in Arkansas, doing who-knows-what. Thank God for appletinis. I'm getting really good at mixing them.

Julie

Julie,

David's nightmares are getting worse. He fell out of bed 2 nights ago. He has nightmares almost every morning between 4 and 6. I wonder (but not really) if they're connected to the late night phone calls from the mutants?

Kerry

Ker,

I hope David is learning to bounce.

Julie

Dear Kerry,

Just checking my emails after 2 days of neglect. Got one for you: Kevin finally confronted his daughter Trisha about the $2000 she owes us. He sent her an email saying he's so glad she's buying an expensive dog, having her house painted, buying a new computer and flying her daughter home (from where she lives with her dad) every month, etc..... But he wanted to remind her about that $2000 debt that she promised to have paid off by *last* January.

A $100 check just showed up in the mail stapled to a copy of Kevin's email. Nothing else.

Julie

Julie,

She's not very good at math is she? Or maybe she was so busy shopping that she just wrote the wrong amount on the check by mistake. Yeah, that must be it.

Wonder what you'll get in the mail if he actually cashes it.

Kerry

33

Getting His Life Together and Tearing Ours Apart

In season 1, episode 20 of *Criminal Minds,* titled "Charm and Harm," a man is traveling through the Southeast, torturing and then drowning women. The F.B.I.'s behavior analysis unit, led by Jason Gideon, must visit the man's father twice in order to get the real story of the killer's childhood. It appears the boy was indulged and protected by his father, who made excuses for his petty crimes and even for statutory rape.

> Gideon: Did Mark ever have to take responsibility for anything?
>
> Father: What are you saying? That being a protective parent has turned my child into a killer?
>
> Gideon: I'm saying you're making excuses and I'm not sure you did him any favors.

I nearly jumped off the couch when I was watching that episode. There it is: consequences. If there are no consequences and your parents make excuses for your bad behavior, won't it continue? Won't it escalate?

After Bryan flunked out of college, because he said his roommate's alcohol problems were so bad that he couldn't concentrate enough to study, he moved in with Pizza Boy. This is when David put out the most money for alcohol and cigarettes. He was giving Bryan money to live on and paying Pizza Boy's rent for the inconvenience of having Bryan live with him. And of course, Nationwide was on their side too. After all, we had to insure those cars we *gave* to them.

Six months went by before Bryan decided he needed to get his life together. Unfortunately, he decided it would be a good idea to do that with David and me in Florida. He said it was hard to be around his sister because she's an alcoholic, and he couldn't stand being around his mother and brother either. By process of elimination, we won. My 84-year-old dad was already living with us after spending years with my brother's family.

David actually asked me what I thought about taking Bryan in. I was blindly accommodating because *I thought* I could finally do some good because *I thought* the kid was at rock bottom. But he wasn't. He was still playing the system.

I told David, "He gets less than a year. He must work and finish school and you control his money so that he has something saved to get an apartment when I kick him out." David agreed and told Bryan to come on down.

To get ready for Bryan's visit, I told David I wanted to store all our liquor bottles at a neighbor's house. He said that wasn't necessary, but if I wanted to get them out of sight, I should just put them in his closet in the master bedroom. I still boxed up most of the bottles and brought them to a neighbor's house. Although I left my wine rack intact. It had just three or four unopened, corked bottles. Oh, and I left one and a half bottles of marsala wine in the pantry. I only use that when I make chicken marsala. Nobody actually drinks marsala wine, or so I thought.

We keep our bar stocked for the occasional party or we stock up when David finds something on sale. God forbid we should miss a sale on his Bloody Mary mix or vodka. So we just happened to have three unopened half gallon bottles of vodka, which David himself valued enough to put among his winter clothes in the large plastic bins in his closet.

Bryan and Jack drove down in Bryan's car and Jack flew back home after a few days. Bryan supposedly had no money. By this time, Jack knew that alcohol was a problem and tried to keep Bryan from getting it. The Daddy Welfare payments to Connecticut went to Jack, with the understanding that he would provide for Bryan. Jack bought the food and cigarettes, but obviously Bryan had been stealing from somewhere because he wasn't leading a sober life.

When Jack left, Bryan took off in his car every day, supposedly to find a job. He also said he was "looking into going to school here in Florida." This went on for a couple of weeks. I tried to stay busy during that time and give Bryan his space. He abused his freedom. I started finding things missing, like the loose change we absentmindedly toss into the trays on our bureaus. Or the GPS navigation device I took out of my father's truck and put in a drawer because Dad didn't go anywhere without me. And didn't I have more than one bottle in the wine rack? I started doubting myself at first.

Then I took a good look at Bryan. It was obvious he was doing nothing but drinking. Of course convincing David of that was another matter. I needed hard evidence and Bryan was becoming a master at manipulating his father, even when drunk. David didn't see it. Probably because he didn't want to. To help him see it, I searched the guest room Bryan was staying in while he was out with David. I found empty liquor bottles everywhere. And I had to search – under the mattress, behind boxes in the closet, under clothes in bureau drawers. Bottles of all sizes, minis to half-gallons, were uncovered everywhere. It was hard for me to believe one person could consume so much alcohol in just the couple of weeks he was here. I also went into David's closet and checked for the three half-gallon bottles of vodka. Two were empty and the other was missing. Next, I took inventory of the wine rack – empty. I know it wasn't empty two weeks ago. Then the pantry, where

I found that there would be no chicken marsala for dinner until I bought a new bottle of marsala wine. Everything was gone. To drink all that, he must have started early every morning and continued late into the evening. He had to have gotten money somehow. There were several empty gin bottles and we don't buy gin.

I took all the empty bottles and piled them on Bryan's bed. As soon as he and David got home, I asked David to follow him into his room. He did and came out looking white as a ghost. He either had no clue, or was reluctant to believe he was going through this with his third child also. He came to me and I told him that wasn't all. I asked David to check out those three half-gallon vodka bottles in his closet. He insisted, even at that moment, that Bryan would never go into his closet. I led the way and David took the empty bottles and finally confronted Bryan angrily, demanding to know why he would go into his closet.

That was it for me. I had to take control because David just didn't get it. Bryan would do anything to find a drink. It wasn't an invasion of privacy issue, it was an alcoholic issue. I got them both in the car and took them to a local hospital for what I hoped would be several days of detox for Bryan and a hard dose of reality for David. Once again, I was wrong. Bryan was evaluated in the emergency room and convinced the doctor that he just drank too much and it wouldn't happen again. Of course that was all David wanted to hear, that it was over and he wouldn't do it again. He was satisfied, back in that Land of Denial.

In the several hours we spent in the ER, a male nurse attended Bryan. Once he realized I was the stepmother, the nurse took me aside and said, "He's playing you, you know." I said I knew. The problem was getting my husband to realize it. He sympathized with me and told me it was going to be a big problem because once a person is over 18, you can't commit him unless you can prove he's going to harm himself or someone else. Drinking to harm himself didn't count, so the nurse warned me we were in for a long battle.

Over the next few days, Bryan told his father that he probably needed to do something like join the army. David saw it as a turning point and started looking up the local recruiting offices for him. I feared for our country, yet hoped he'd find some service that would take him, and a satanic drill sergeant who would break him during basic training. Bryan actually went through with a few visits to the offices David found and he started to talk seriously about the future. He even took some of the online tests the recruiters suggested, and he did well.

I know a National Guard recruiter from my teaching days and I asked him to pay us a visit so David and I could be in on one of these recruiting conversations. Sergeant Ramos came to our home and did a great job of selling, assuring Bryan that once he got in, he'd have a purpose that would inspire him to make it a career. I could see the hope in David's eyes. But I also read Bryan. He wanted no part of this. He was just playing us again, giving us something to think about so that we wouldn't stay focused on his demeanor and behavior.

Just two days after this visit, Bryan came home drunk and enraged. He went into his room and took a knife to the Lazy Boy recliner we had recently bought. David went after him and I heard yelling and threats from Bryan. He kept saying to David, "I'm going to kill you." Later David would tell me that Bryan was holding the knife to his throat and David had to wrestle it away from him. He also told me, much later, that it was not the first time that had happened on this visit.

I called 911. When David came out and realized I was on the phone with the sheriff's office, he demanded that I hang up and said he would take care of the situation. Not this time buddy. I told the dispatcher what my husband said and she insisted I stay on the phone with her and go outside. I did. David followed me into the driveway and Bryan wasn't far behind. Now Bryan was yelling that he was going to kill me too. Lovely.

Must have been a great show for the neighbors. David trying to take the phone away from me, Bryan yelling, and me repeating every word to the dispatcher. Thank God the sheriff's deputy arrived. He saw me on the phone and realized I was the one who called 911. Bryan went back into the house and David tried to tell the deputy that there was no need for him to be there.

David: Officer, it's just my son. He got out of hand
              because he's drunk, but I can handle him.

Deputy: Sir, step aside. Your wife is the one who called. I'm
              working for her.

David: But everything's okay.

Deputy: Sir, step aside or I'll take you in too.

David knew he was serious and let me do the rest of the talking. I told the deputy everything I had heard Bryan say, and I asked him to please get him out of my house.

The deputy went inside and found Bryan in his room. In the meantime, David told me that I shouldn't have called the police and I told him to shut up or my friend the deputy would be getting 2-for-1 on this call. He knew I was serious too, so this time, he wisely shut up. I could see that he was even glad to be relinquishing control. Even though he said he'd handle it, he really had no plan and no clue as to how to subdue a violent drunk who was threatening to kill us in our own home.

The deputy was incredible in this situation. I had seen officers like him before, handling troubled kids at school. They truly are amazing, patient, and well-educated in psychology. They're also strong and agile enough to take down an uncooperative drunk. After about a half hour, he took Bryan out, calm and in handcuffs. David was crying, but I don't know if it was the sight of his son going off to the big house or the relief that someone else was finally imposing the consequences that he never could. The deputy put him into the back of the patrol car and told us he was going to Baker Act him. That means, hold him in a hospital for 72 hours because he's a danger to himself and others. After that, it was likely that he would be free and we needed to find some place for him to go.

David seemed to be glad that he was going to a hospital instead of jail. He still hoped that some doctor could fix him in 72 hours. I knew they'd get him sober, but that's about it. The drunken downward spiral would start again as soon as he got out.

During the hospital lock up, David went alone to visit Bryan. He also got information about follow-up procedures and he chose an in-patient facility here in the Orlando area. David told Bryan he would have to sign himself in for at least two weeks if he ever wanted our help to get well. Bryan agreed. However, once he got there, he disagreed. Fortunately, this was after he signed in and David left, so he had nowhere to go and no way to get there. He was stuck and David let him stay stuck for whatever reason, probably exhaustion. David's, not Bryan's.

Bryan complained the whole time he was at the facility. He said the other people there were all "druggies" and he was not like "those people." Of course the doctors had a different opinion, so we let him experience being around "those people" for a couple of weeks. He hated it. Welcome to my world, Bryan. I refer to people like you as "those people" too.

David and I had somewhat of a rest during those two weeks because visits were not allowed. We started planning for the aftermath.

I decided Bryan would not be spending another minute in our house, so his mother helped search for an in-patient facility in Connecticut. She found one, as far away from her place as is geographically possible. But at least she found one. They couldn't take him until one week after he was being let out of his current facility in Orlando.

I told David to pick a hotel where he might like to spend a week with Bryan. I refused to let him back into our home, even for the week. We live 30 minutes from Disney World. The choices are endless. But my *moneybags* husband chose the cheapest place he could find. It was less than 20 miles away and it was a bargain at $129 a week. Looking back, he probably wishes he opened his wallet a little wider. Room service, a pool, or at least HBO would have been nice. Instead, they stayed in that economy-priced room together for one solid week, except for hitting the fast-food places for meals. David said Bryan talked and talked about how miserable he was, but blamed everyone else for his problems. So much for group therapy with "those people." Same old Bryan. And now David saw it for himself. He finally understood that Bryan turned out to be exactly like his mother, brother and sister.

I spent the week packing up Bryan's personal belongings. I put everything in boxes and taped them up like mummies so David wouldn't have anything to rummage through to slow him down before that trip to the airport. He warned me he was coming home to pack up a few things. So I put clothes and some other items in a suitcase to toss in the car as he drove by. He didn't even have to come to a full stop. As my dear friend Joan would say, "I already took care of it dear."

When the plane took off with a sober, but still enraged Bryan, David came home and collapsed. He needed a drink, but chose to sleep instead. That was fine. More for me! I found time to re-stock the bar during my week off. I didn't even wait for the sales.

Bryan's brother Jack picked him up from the airport and took him to the rehab place in Connecticut. Not Bucky. Imagine that.

From Jack's description and our online research, we knew it was a large facility that housed both drunks and druggies. After a few days, Bryan told David it was not the right place for him. There were more of "those people." Just like his father, the patient insisted he knew what was best. It's times like these that I am reminded of the simple genius of Oprah's Dr. Phil. "Take a good look at where your way has gotten you. How's that workin' for ya?"

When Bryan finished his expensive rehab vacation, he went back to Jack's apartment and the drunken cycle began all over again, just as I predicted. *(Don't be impressed. A monkey could have made the same prediction.)* Bryan did nothing for two years. No job. No school. Nothing. To quote myself, "He didn't have to." Jack continued his pizza delivery job. David continued to subsidize both of them and Jack was on his way to becoming a full-fledged enabler like his father.

Back in Florida, David used a little more self-control in discussing money with me and only mentioned my spending when he noticed something obvious like the $2,500 king size Tempurpedic mattress on our bed. I was tired of his restlessness and nightmares affecting my sleep. So I believed that commercial where the glass of red wine doesn't spill even though the wife is jumping on the bed while the husband is reclining. David's nightmares were so violent that he'd be flailing all over the place and he often fell out of bed with a *thud* before waking up. The commercial was true to a point. I was still able to drink my full glass of red wine in bed, without spilling it, but I never slept through the whole night without feeling David thrashing. And the *thud* always woke me up. The mattress was returned and David only had the $75 return shipping fee to cry about.

34

What, Us Worry?

When Julie and I got married to Kevin and David, the 20 and 15 year age differences were not much of a factor in our day-to-day existence. Women in their 30s and men in their 50s can be pretty compatible if they're in good health. The four of us have been blessed with good health.

Now it's about 20 years later and the men are hovering near 70 and we're in our 50s. The stress from dealing with *the children* has taken it's toll on all of us.

Julie and I worry constantly that the offspring are taking years off our husbands' lives. We're pretty much resolved to the fact that we're going to be widows someday. We've talked about it. We've even got plans to go on a singles' cruise together. Julie says she won't inform the girls about Kevin's demise until it's too late for them to pounce at any funeral event. I like that idea. If David died tomorrow, I'd wait a good week and a half before I let the word get to anyone in Connecticut. Julie and I have taken enough. We're not going to watch the crocodile tears from the sponges at the time of our losses. They can wait to get their checks.

Although the men aren't ready to kick the bucket, they have had their health problems. Nothing devastating or fatal, but aches and pains common to men of their age. There have been a few operations and invasive tests over the past few years. And when the doctors advise them to "take it easy," all Julie and I can do is smile knowingly. There is no "easy" at this end of the phone lines, emails, texts, whatever. Any pain our husbands suffer with is compounded by intrusions from the *kids* about their own problems. "I'm sorry you're not feeling well Dad but...."

Julie and I have some medical issues too. Nothing that can't be managed, but it would be nice if the problems weren't exacerbated by stress.

Menopause was a real fun time for me. In an easy-going, low-key environment, it's no picnic. I know that from some of my single and widowed girlfriends. But imagine the hot flashes, weight gain and mood swings added to my fun-house world. Holy shit! Someone could have gotten hurt. David and I don't keep weapons around, but Kevin is a hunter. He's had to double check that locked gun safe on my trips to Jackson. I swear, if I ever had a gun during one of the episodes with the mutants, while I was having a hot flash, I would have used it. I'm not sure whom I would have shot, but I would have shot someone. Instead, I write, the pen being mightier and all. I've even started a fictional screenplay version of this book which starts off with Julie and I in adjoining cells, doing not-so-hard-time for offing the offspring.

Throughout my marriage I've grown very fond of t.v. crime shows like *NCIS, CSI,* and especially *Criminal Minds*. David accuses me of watching for research. I tell him, "That's crazy." But really, it's not that crazy. He knows by now that if I did kill one of his kids, a jury of *my peers* (women married to enablers) would call it justifiable homicide.

The crime shows I like always end happily. I mean, there *is* justice, even if it's only implied. I don't like some episodes of *Law & Order* because the good guy doesn't always win. In my world, the good guy wins all the time. Maybe that's another reason why I've stayed. I know I'll win my husband away from the evil demons that stalk him. It's just taking longer than I thought.

There are times when I want to talk to David about our marriage and how we're not exactly living the life we had planned when we retired to Florida. But in that conversation, I have to bring up the fact that he is still an enabler and that always upsets him. I try to do this calmly, thinking I can ease him out of his behavior if I can ease him into trying to live a happier and healthier lifestyle. It doesn't work. Just talking about the dependency issues of all three of his wayward brats makes David react with, "Look, I'm shaking already. You're upsetting me." Then he'll get out his automatic blood pressure machine and give me his readings. So I have to stop. But not before I leave him with one thought: "You have the power. If your behavior changed, so would theirs." Then he walks away and life goes on. Nope, nothing to worry about here.

35

Freedom and Independence

"Kerry Ann, you'd better learn to take care of yourself because no one else is going to do it for you."

– Dad

That's what my father said to me over the phone as I cried to him from 3,000 miles away. I was in Bakersfield, California, at my first real job after college. I was 21. I expected him to tell me to come home if I was so miserable. He didn't. He encouraged me to stay and wrote me a letter nearly every week. None of those letters contained a check or a plane ticket. So I continued in a television news and sports reporting job at an NBC television station, making a whopping $14,500 a year in 1981. And you know what? I survived. Actually, I *learned* to survive. Dad was right and now I had something to be proud of. I worked my way out of that job because he wouldn't let me whine my way out of it. That's what dads are supposed to do.

"Kerry, you've got to have cash. You have to keep at least $10,000 available at all times. If I have to leave immediately, I want to have the means to live while I decide what to do next."

– Patricia

That's what my friend Patty advised me to do when David's enabling of his children first became an issue. She kept her nest egg hidden in her closet. Like me and Julie, Patty is married to an older man with money who enables his kids. There are so many of *them* out there. And hey, there are so many of *us* out there too. Imagine what we could do if we harness this strength in numbers. We might be able to save at least one child. But until then, Patty thought there might be a day when she would want to run away. The $10,000 in cash was part of her escape plan.

"Marry a man with money and you'll earn every penny of it."

– Greg

That's a warning from my friend Greg. We worked together and shared stories of his kids and my stepkids. His stories were pretty bad, but mine were worse. He's right about the earning. Being married to David is the toughest job I've ever had. And David isn't even what I'd call *rich*, just secure. I mean, it's not like he has his own plane or anything. I've dated guys with planes. Julie's husband has a plane. David has a Southwest Airlines frequent flier card.

Now that I'm older and wiser, when I see millionaires being divorced by their young wives, I don't judge as harshly as other people. If those women are fed up enough to divorce a man they planned to spend the rest of their lives with, they probably earned most, if not all, of what they're going to get. Money doesn't solve problems, it skews them.

To those on the outside, I'm sure it looked like I was acquiring a lot by marrying David. So much, in fact, that no one would have thought I was giving up anything. Not even me. But I was. And I don't mean my life as a carefree bachelorette. I mean my financial independence.

When you're 37 years old and getting married for the first and *only* time, maybe your priorities are a little off-the-mark when it comes to lifestyle. I quickly forgot about how I had lived on a budget and eased into our life together in a higher tax bracket. I wasn't really thinking about money and I valued our partnership more than I valued my independence. Maybe I didn't think I'd need my independence anymore. I made it all the way to 37 without help. I didn't have anything to prove. Together, David and I could afford a better lifestyle than I had alone, so why hold on to my independence? I'll tell you why.

I went from a $600-a-month apartment in a blue collar town to a $695,000 mortgage-free home at the end of a long gravel driveway, down a dirt road, off a cul-de-sac in a rich and snooty neighborhood where no one mowed their own lawns or cleaned their own bathrooms and everyone's pets had pedigrees.

I once asked a neighbor if I could hire her teenage kids to care for our non-pedigreed cats while we were away. She said, "My kids don't need money. They use my credit cards." I certainly wish I kept in touch with her, just to see how those credit-card kids turned out. I'll bet she's got enough stories to write a book. Or, if she got divorced, I hope her ex-husband's new wife finds this book before she gets hit by the freight train fueled by those credit cards.

The first time my friend, Rosanne, visited our grand, or rather, grandiose house, she stood on the marble floor of the foyer, beneath the crystal chandelier, looking into the living room and said, "Geez, you could put a bowling alley in here." Yep, you could. But then I asked her, "Who would really bowl in this neighborhood, besides us?"

Our house was what David had to show from his divorce. He took his half of the settlement and built this house as an investment. It hadn't sold yet, so we moved into it. We knew it was much too big for us, but we were toughing it out. Don't laugh. It was tough. David mowed. I cleaned bathrooms. We both shoveled a whole lot of snow off that gravel driveway. We don't pay for things we're perfectly capable of doing ourselves.

My teacher's salary would rise steadily over our next ten years in Connecticut. And David went back to work in the mortgage business for a few years. We eventually made a lot of money on the sale of that house, invested it, and moved into a more appropriate neighborhood for our means and values. As I said earlier, David and I were a team and with his experience as a banker, I was fine with letting him handle the money.

As a new wife, I didn't anticipate big problems. After all, I was 37 and he was 52. That maturity was my assurance that we both knew what we were doing. So it came as a huge surprise to me, that at least twice during that first year, I had the kind of meltdown that made me want to escape. I actually thought about getting a divorce. That's when I realized my friend Patty's plan had some merit, Greg's warning was an accurate prediction, and my father overestimated my ability to survive.

If I had $10,000 in cash hidden in my closet, I would have left. I would have gone somewhere, anywhere away from the chaos, gotten my head together and.... And what? I might have come back. I might have hired a divorce lawyer. Maybe my escape would have been a catalyst to trigger David to acquire some parenting skills right then and there, rather than lose me for good.

Well, who really knows what I would have done? But I do know this: even a few moments of peace at those meltdown times would have done me a world of good. With $10,000 in cash, designated for the purpose of getting away, I could have spent a couple of nights in a nice hotel, taken advantage of an in-room massage, maybe gone shopping. Without the cash, I felt like I couldn't go because I didn't have a license to spend *our* money to get away from *our* marriage. It's psychological, I know. I mean, I could have used a credit card, written a check, or gone to the bank. But the immediacy of cash-on-hand imparts freedom of choice. I didn't prepare like Patty did. Instead, I stayed and suffered, hoping either my attitude or the circumstances would change. I was reluctant to consider divorce so early in my marriage and so late in my life. I had to stay and fix it.

After much therapy and medication, I think differently now. Patty's plan is a good one. Greg's "earning" makes me diligent and

I can take something positive from that. And dad's lesson resonates because I've learned that "taking care of myself" does not mean I have to stay put. Now I escape when I need to.

I must admit I still don't keep $10,000 cash in my pajama drawer. It doesn't earn any interest there and I would rather have the interest than the instant access. But I know the limits on my credit cards and I'm not afraid to use them to get away and save my sanity when the shit hits the fan.

Sometimes I go to Connecticut to see my dad, my hairdresser and some old friends. Sometimes I go to Sarasota to do yoga with Joyce. Sometimes I just fill the tank and drive. But I have the most fun when I take one of my little vacations in Jackson, with Julie.

36

I'm Going to Jackson

That Johnny Cash-June Carter hit, *Jackson*, was a favorite of mine when I was a kid. Not for any reason other than it was a catchy tune. One of the reasons I was glad to move from Connecticut to Florida is that now Jackson is only a short plane ride, or a mere 12-hour drive away.

I'm goin' to Jackson, I'm gonna mess around,
Yeah, I'm goin' to Jackson,
Look out Jackson town.

I took off for Jackson to stay at Julie and Kevin's when David invited his boys to come for a visit. The 12-hour drive might have intimidated some, but for me, it was half a day of blissful peace or National Public Radio ("that goddamned liberal station," according to David) or country music, rock, jazz, comedy, books-on-tape or anything else I chose to come out of the car speakers. It was my time.

David and I decided the summer of 2010 would be our time to travel. We had been through a lot the previous fall with Bryan threatening to kill us and all. And in January, Don Mattingly died (the dog, not the baseball player). So dogless and nervous, we decided to take two vacations, one planned by David and one planned by me.

When I found out that David invited Pizza Boy Jack down for a week in between, I decided to take three vacations.

Yeah, I'm goin' to Jackson.

Our first trip together was to a lovely all-inclusive resort in Puerto Plata, Dominican Republic. It's on the north shore, closest to Haiti where a hurricane had just hit and elections were about to be held. There was plenty of political unrest and violence occurring at the time. David found the place on one of his bargain websites which didn't mention the current climate. When he figured out the cost-per-hour (minute or whatever), he said we had to go for two weeks because we couldn't live as cheaply at home as we could at this resort. One week cost $1,450 and two weeks was a bargain, according to him, at $1,850.

It was okay, considering. Considering the beach was too rocky for swimming and it wasn't safe to leave the resort. But hey, the price of captivity was too cheap to pass up. And isn't that what's really important when you're trying to relax? Two freakin' weeks of sun, food, drinks and David, surrounded by protests and criminal activity. Funny, we didn't run into another Floridian the whole time. I guess most Floridians already have enough sun, pools and beach. I read all four books I brought with me, the three others in the hotel library that were printed in English, and I still had about five days to go.

We met some nice people from the Midwest, several couples around our age. They all had children in college, or who had just graduated, and they told wonderful stories about the college years. David was quiet except to say he had a son at UCONN. He didn't mention that the son is a violent drunk who hardly passed half of his classes, never took a full load, flunked out and didn't have a job. Listening to the others, I had to wonder if they were telling the truth. I mean, what were the chances of having four or five couples in a cold tub (no need for hot tubs when it's over 100 degrees and sunny every day), drinking lots of top shelf liquor, talking about successful college kids and being the only couple without one? I really don't know, but this scenario repeats itself often, even at home, sans the cold tub and tropical drinks. I haven't dared to ask, but I wonder what David thinks about when he hears how others are moving on with their retirement lives without choosing to support their grown children who are successful on their own.

After our sun and fun adventure in the D.R., I had two days at home before I got back on the road to Jackson as Jack headed down to Florida with the plane ticket bought by you-know-who. David validated this purchase by saying that Jack was coming down to drive Bryan's car home because Bryan couldn't drive it home when he left here last fall because, well, you know, the handcuffs, murder threats, lack of sobriety and all. The car had been parked in our driveway ever since.

This was my old Toyota Camry, which we gave Bryan at the end of his sophomore year in college because he was moving into an apartment off campus because of his shy bladder. The car was in perfect condition and very clean when we let it go. Now it was dented all around, smelled of cigarettes and more (shy bladder, my ass!), was full of garbage and looked like a bum was living in it. Proves my point that a *free* car had no value to a kid who didn't have to work and spend his own money to get it.

I was so glad that Julie would be home that week to welcome me back to Jackson. And there was a bonus. That weekend, Greg Olson Night was scheduled at Trustmark Park, the minor league ballpark in Pearl, Mississippi. Greg used to play for the Jackson Mets when I was covering sports back in the mid '80s. After the Mets traded him, he became a star as the catcher for the Atlanta Braves. I hadn't seen him in over 20 years, so I figured that alone was worth the trip. A friend of mine and Julie's, Johnny Maloney, had another friend with a luxury suite booked at the ballpark that evening, so we were going first class. Well, first class for Pearl. The burgers and beer were free.

Julie went home after the game, but with Johnny and Greg, I had a new audience and they had some baseball stories to tell. The three of us went over to the local Hilton Hotel bar and told stories until closing. Johnny's brother owned the Jackson Mets, the double-A team for the New York Mets, during the early 1980s when a lot of the 1986 Mets World Series superstars were coming up. Plenty of those guys lived at Johnny's house when they played in Jackson. Johnny has a great memory for those at-home stories. Like the one about the guy who slept with his bat and the one about the guy whose girlfriend had the same first name as his wife. That was pretty convenient. Greg had a ton of great stories too, from his time in the big leagues. He was on the Braves during the years that outfielder David Justice was married to actress Halle Berry. I'll leave those stories for Greg's book. But let's just say that, except for the celebrity factor, my stories of Pizza Boy, Drunk Girl and Violent Drunk Boy, and how they were financed, got just as many laughs. The evening was inspirational to the writer in me. Thanks guys.

I was also glad to have the opportunity to spend some time with my old friend Christopher that weekend. He was having a tumultuous time since he graduated from Jackson State. He was taking post-graduate classes towards his master's degree in public administration and that was going well. But the company he worked for moved out of state. So except for some seasonal part-time jobs, he was unemployed. He kept busy going on interviews, using the library for job searches and the bus lines for transportation. He did some landscaping work for cash and he also worked as a barber for friends. He turned his love of cooking into a job too because people were willing to pay. He was that good. I couldn't wait to tell David how wonderfully he was handling his unemployment dilemma.

The first thing Christopher did when he got laid off was to pay up his rent for a full year so he wouldn't have to worry about it. He's a devotee of Suzy Orman and her financial teachings and he had an emergency fund built up and ready. Imagine that. And at such a young age. I'll bet David would have done that too. Couldn't wait to tell him.

Except for a gift for his college graduation, I had never given Christopher cash. I once took him shopping for school clothes years ago and I also took him grocery shopping during one of my visits when his mother was alive. She made out the list and we stuck to it. The charity that put us together stressed that we should send our families essential items, but not cash, and I followed the rules. However I wanted to help out a little now, so I suggested a trip to the grocery store at my expense. Oh my God! He shopped like David. He compared prices, bought items on sale, mostly meats, only essentials, and no junk. I didn't set a limit, but he spent just $70. Yep, couldn't wait to tell David.

So after a few relaxing days with old friends, Julie's loving pets, good food and wine, it was time to get back on the road to Florida. I thought Pizza Boy would be gone and I'd have a couple of days to clean up the mess in the guest room and the kitchen before David and I got on a plane for the vacation I planned to Mt. Rushmore, Rapid City and the Badlands of South Dakota in the good ol' U.S. of A. Anything but sun, pools, beach and the customs line at the airport.

I called David on the way home and found out Pizza Boy wasn't leaving until the following day. Okay, I could cope with just one day. It might give me the opportunity to share some of my stories about Christopher with him. Maybe it would inspire Pizza Boy to get a real job or a life. There's always hope.

As I got closer to Orlando, I thought about calling to warn David to make sure our garage was empty so I could drive right in after 12 hours on the road. Bryan's smelly car was out in the driveway when I left. There was no reason to move it inside and stink up the garage, or so I thought. David didn't think that way. He just filled the empty space in the garage with the only car left at home. When I saw the empty driveway and hit the garage remote button, I stopped on the street, called David on my cell phone and *politely* asked him to "move that goddamned stinkin' car out of *my* garage." He did and I pulled in. I got the silent treatment for a while after that. He and Pizza Boy were watching a baseball game, so I guess ignoring me and being mad at me looked kind of the same. But I knew.

The next day, as David was getting Jack all ready to drive back to Connecticut, because a 35-year-old *boy* shouldn't have to do that for himself without daddy's help, I sat at the computer to write out my notes for this chapter. That's when the silent treatment ended.

David: Does Bryan's car have a tape player?

Kerry: Are you talking to me?

David: Does Bryan's car have a tape player?

Kerry: Yes, can't you see the hole in the dashboard?

David: Does it work?

Kerry: It did when it was my car without all those dents and that fungus growing inside.

David: Do we have any tapes so I can try it?

Kerry: Yes we do.

David: Where are they?

Kerry: Where they always are, in the cabinet with the CDs.

David: Where's that?

Kerry: *(@#$%$#@*! and getting up to throw a Beach Boys cassette to/at him.)*

Several minutes go by and I hear Jack telling him he needs a CD *converter* for the tape player so that he can play CDs, not an old Beach Boys cassette.

David: The tape player works. Jack needs a converter so he can play his CDs.

Kerry: Okay.

David: Do you have one?

Kerry: Why would I have one?

David: He says it's to play CDs. Don't you play CDs?

Kerry: Yes. Our car has a CD player.

David: So we don't have one?

Kerry: One what?

David: A converter for CDs.

Kerry: We never needed one, so probably not.

More time goes by as they discuss how Jack is going to survive his two-day drive home to Connecticut with just an am/fm radio and a cassette player, plenty of daddy's money for a hotel, food, expenses and gas. Yep, tough trip. Just like the many times I drove up or down the coast in 21 hours straight with David, Don Mattingly (the dog, not the baseball player) my father, Bryan, and boxes full of stuff we were moving to the new house, all without stopping at a hotel. David never drove because his panic attacks and road rage would have killed us all. But hey, he was getting that smelly car out of my life and he was doing it without Bryan anywhere near us, so that was something. I tried to hold on for a few more hours but my wonderful husband didn't make it easy.

David: Do we have a map?

Kerry: Of what?

David: You know of what. So Jack can get home.

Kerry: Wasn't he in the car with Bryan when they came down here? Where's the map he used for that trip?

David: I need a map.

Kerry: We have plenty of them in the map drawer.

David: The map drawer? What map drawer?

Kerry: In the office. The bottom drawer of the file cabinet is full
        of maps.

David: *(Looking through the drawer.)* Which one should I
        give him?

Kerry: If it were me, I'd give him one of the East Coast.

*(I lied. If it were me, I'd give him directions into the heart of the
Bermuda Triangle.)*

There was just one more day at home before we were off to
South Dakota for the one-week vacation I had planned, which David
said cost us three times as much as his two weeks in the Dominican
Republic because "my wife *needs* to stay in the *only* room in the *only*
hotel with a view of that goddamned mountain from our balcony."
Hell, if I didn't have that week to look up at those peaceful, majestic
American heroes carved in stone the first thing in the morning and
the last thing before turning in at night instead of looking at David, I
probably would have killed him in his sleep.

> *"… we believe a nation's memorial should, like Washington,
> Jefferson, Lincoln and Roosevelt, have a serenity, a nobility, a
> power that reflects the gods who inspired them and suggests the
> gods they have become."*
>
> – *Gutzon Borglum*
> *Sculptor of Mt. Rushmore*

37

Memorial Day Weekend Emails

Hey Julie,

Went outside to walk the dog while David was on the phone with one of his kids. Sometimes I don't want to know until I have to. But I knew it was bad because he came out after me. Bryan is in jail for beating up Cindy. She's in the hospital. Jack called to tell David the good news. David told him to leave Bryan in jail. Hmm. That's what I would have said. Then he told me that Jack does too much for Bryan. Hmm. Exactly what I was thinking. He said everything to me about Jack that I've said to him about himself. Duh. Maybe now he gets it? Nah. It's too much to hope for. Happy Freakin' Memorial Day Weekend!!!

Aren't holiday weekends just the best? The very best!

Kerry

Happy Holiday Ker,

So I guess they're gonna miss the big Memorial Day parade. Too bad.

Julie

Hey Julie,

Unfortunately Bryan didn't do a good enough job of beating up Cindy. Drunk Girl keeps calling but we unplugged the phone. However, we have home phone service through our cable company so every time she calls it flashes on the television screen. Geez, if I were going to go to jail for beating someone up, I'd like to think I would have done enough damage to knock her out for a couple of days. How is this going to end?

Kerry

Ker,

It's not going to end good and it's not going to end.

Julie

38

In the News

I have gotten into the habit of looking at the online news section of all the Connecticut newspapers, daily and weekly, around the town where the adult children live. I used to look only at the obituaries to see if there was anyone I knew so I could send a condolence card to the family. But then I realized I would also find familiar names in the police blotter section of the news from time to time. Condolence cards for that crap should come to me.

"Local man faces assault, weapons charges after dispute with woman" was the online headline. And I knew it would explain yesterday's phone calls. It went on to say 23-year-old Bryan punched and kicked a woman several times at her home and then tried to fight his way out of police custody. They didn't actually identify Cindy as his sister and they didn't mention that both of them were drunk. The fight started in the home, according to police, and ended up on the front lawn.

Bryan was combative, according to the report, and had a knife. They also said he attempted to kick out a window in the patrol car and then tried to strike an officer at police headquarters.

Cindy was taken to a local hospital.

Bryan was charged with second-degree assault, carrying a dangerous weapon, interfering with an officer and disorderly conduct.

He was released after Pizza Boy called Daddy and begged for money so he could post $5,000 bond.

So that's how it appeared in the newspaper, except for that last sentence about Pizza Boy, which I added. And yes, Jack convinced David to give him the money to get Bryan out of jail even though David's first instinct was to leave him there.

Bryan and Cindy were both drunk and out of control more times than not. Bryan had been living with his brother Jack and doing nothing but taking a class or two for several years. Cindy was always unemployed and living with her mother. The apartments were close enough so that, even drunk, they could find their way from one to the other. Mom's place was usually where the two of them got wasted while she was at work. Then the fights would start. Physical fights, not just arguments. This one spilled outside and the neighbors reported it.

Daily newspapers have been sadly disappearing all over the country and there are less than half of what there were in Connecticut when I was growing up. One daily that has survived is the Connecticut Post. They run a weekly sports history column. During baseball, softball and basketball seasons, a search for my husband's last name would pull up his accomplishments from the big games back in the day, 30 or 40 years ago. It was fun for both of us to read about his youth. But these days, a search for his last name in that online newspaper brings up more than his game-winning scores. It brings up the arrest records of his children. They've ruined that for him too.

39

Near Death Without Missing School

Bryan's court case was scheduled at the end of June. That gave Jack one month to try and get his brother sober. It wasn't nearly enough time. As Jack was dealing with a drunken Bryan, Bucky was manipulating her drunken daughter, who was quite a mess from the beating. Bucky convinced her to drop the charges against her brother. All he would be going to court for now would be the the assault on the police officer and the weapons charge.

I guess the police gave that knife back to Bryan when Jack came to pick him up with daddy's money for bail. And Bryan wasn't through using it. It took a couple of days but he didn't stop drinking and eventually trashed Jack's apartment and cut Jack while fighting with that knife. That was it for Jack's babysitting service. He threw him out. Of course Jack's next step was to call both Mommy and Daddy to tell them he threw him out. Daddy said, "Good for you." Really, he did. Bucky, on the other hand, took Bryan in to live with her and her drunken daughter, the same one Bryan tried to kill. Talk about a perfect storm.

We had about one week of silence, the calm before the storm, and then both drunks started another cycle of madness.

Bryan was drinking non-stop, using student loan money we wouldn't find out about until months later. He was out on the street or in a bar when he wasn't at his mom's apartment. Cindy was drinking non-stop at home.

Bucky got fed up after a few days and chose Cindy over Bryan, as usual, and kicked him out. She gave him money so that he could go to a hotel. She also called the police, recognizing that another crisis was probably inevitable. The police tracked him down on the street and, fortunately for him, they found him before he died of alcohol poisoning. He was in the hospital for five days of detox, which coincidentally were five non-school days before the first summer semester. He had signed up for two college classes as a commuter.

Those five days were almost peaceful for us, except for the calls from Cindy. She told both of us she was afraid to stay at home if Bryan was coming back. We told her to go to a shelter. But she said she was going to move in with Jack and get a job. We thought about warning Jack, but figured that after she slept off her current binge, she wouldn't remember her plan anyway. We were right.

Bucky kept Jack in the loop about the hospital detox. That's how we got our information on Bryan. We hoped that facing death would have some impact on him. Maybe he'd finally try Alcoholics Anonymous or some other 12-step or out-patient program on his own. He was still on his mother's insurance, so another in-house facility was not out of the question either. He got out of the hospital on a Monday and went back to his mother's place. On Tuesday, he went to the satellite branch of UCONN and went to class. His week-long adventure that ended in detox and included knifing his brother, getting thrown out by both Jack and his mother, drinking until he passed out, and an ambulance ride to the hospital, seemed to be nothing more than a bump in the road to him. He said he was back in school and didn't need any help with his drinking. Well, that's true. Kind of. He's fully capable of drinking on his own. It's the stopping part that he seems to need help with.

The judge in Bryan's case from the Memorial Day weekend adventure, in a his infinite wisdom I'm sure, decided that Bryan should attend some kind of anger management and alcohol classes. So, as you can imagine, school was finally full-time, for a few weeks. Lots and lots of classes. But nothing changed. It took about four months for Bryan to get sick and tired of taking refuge at Bucky's. He made up with his brother and, despite David's warning to Jack, Jack took him in again.

David and I did some talking at this point. David was finally making sense, telling me that Jack should not take Bryan in. He should just leave him alone. He also told me he would not be giving them any money. I don't remember his exact words, so I'm thinking he said it in a way to leave himself a loophole to give them money while still *not lying* to me. Who knows? And at this point, who cares?

For the moment, I tried to enjoy the thought that David's enabling days might be coming to an end. Then I called Julie to update her and she set me straight. It was false hope rearing its ugly head. Silly me, again.

She told me that after Tracey died, it was peaceful for a while until Kevin started going over and over what he *didn't do* for her. I didn't understand. From my point of view, he did too much for her, as David does for his kids. That's why she never learned to take care of herself. Julie agreed. But even in hindsight, his view is that he failed her because he didn't do enough.

They'll never see it objectively, Kevin and David. They can't. They can't see that which would break them. Their survival skills are different from ours and they don't translate.

40

Happy, but not so much, Birthday Dad!

This email from Bryan was sent at 7 a.m., the day after David's birthday in August. They were on the phone together, just 6 hours earlier. Bryan was still at his mother's place after trashing his brother's apartment.

(Author's note: Grammar, punctuation and spelling errors have been corrected for easier reading.)

Dear Dad,

I'm sorry for the way I acted over the phone, but as you can see I've been living a healthier lifestyle just by looking at the time I sent this email. Early to bed, early to rise. With Jack I could never have done that. He passes out at 4 a.m., wakes up at 1 or 2 p.m., smokes pot all day long, takes painkillers with his coffee when he wakes up and when he comes home from work. *He needs help*, but usually only on the brink of disaster do people make great changes. Hopefully Jack will learn this when he gets arrested for selling felony drugs.

He has no shame and feels no guilt. He will do whatever it takes to get what Jack thinks he "needs."

You can believe me or not. Frankly I don't care. Of course, Jack will deny everything, but I know him better than anyone. I took care of him at Emma's, pushed him in a wheelchair around Stop and Shop, and listened to his constant complaining over the last six years. I couldn't stay there anymore. He filled me with hate. With Mom, I finally have peace. A release from the negativity weighed down on me by living with Jack. Let me just give you a small list of the things he's done. First off he only went to court with me once, but I didn't need him anyway. The last few times I've gone on my own. I'm not loaded with fear like my siblings.

But one big problem I had is that he used me to get money from you. I hardly ate anything remotely expensive. We're talking Elio's cheap frozen pizza and pasta. Sure, he cooked nice dinners, but he always bought things fresh. He never shopped wisely. Even when we had the chance to use mom's BJ's card so we could get things at a big discount, things we used a lot (coffee, juice, olive oil, bottled water because he refused to drink from the tap, just to name a few). Not to mention we both were getting food stamps equaling $400 a month. He was able to pull that off because he gets paid under the table, but you may have already known that.

He lied to Cindy about the job interview she went to yesterday for the sole purpose of getting her nervous and disappointed. He dented the hood of my car and told mom to tell me that I did it while I was drunk, which is impossible because I never got to use my car. His car was sitting in his friend's driveway since last October, and he made excuse after excuse to not get it fixed so he could use my car, which he is still using. Although he is finally getting it fixed, but in mom's driveway, of course. Just another tactic he uses to upset Cindy.

Now, to the student loan. I don't know why I took it out, I guess I thought Jack and I could use the money, especially after my arrest. I trusted him with that money so I wouldn't spend it foolishly, and when I wanted it back so I could give it to Mom to help fix the car that was running on a donut in the front-right, and pay for my own expenses like cigarettes, which I've been cutting down by staying away from your junkie of a son. Then he had the balls to keep $2,800 and only give me back $2,000 when I'm using it to help MY family.

Do you spend time with your family? Because a man who doesn't spend time with his family can never be a real man.

Anyways, I'm sorry again. I should have wished you a happy birthday sooner, but then again, you've forgotten mine on several occasions. I don't take it personally. I'm not mad at you. I'll always love you, but I want you to wake up and see Jack for who he really is.

I know him better than anyone after living with him all that time, watching him lie constantly, and basically using anyone around him. That's all he does! He manipulates and takes advantage of people. That's why he has no REAL friends.

I'm sorry to break this to you, but maybe you should come back to Connecticut without telling Jack and see the way he lives. I've begged him to go to doctors, but it's no use. It's like he wants to die.

This all may sound harsh, but I need to make it clear that Jack is cruel, manipulative, and a pathological liar. I'm pretty sure Kerry has known it all along. And years ago after he went to the hospital for nearly drinking himself to death, he replaced it with something even worse: synthetic heroin. Unless he gets really sick again or ends up in jail, I don't see any hope for him.

I know this is tough, but you need to break down that wall of denial. Jack is not your friend. He is your son, and he's been getting away with murder for far too long.

And I don't need your help anymore, and I would prefer that we stick to emails since your voice only upsets me. You're too moody, but that's not your fault. Still, you need to do some growing up too, Old Man. I'm no saint, but I know I'm smarter than you.

I love you, Dad, and I appreciate all you've done and tried to do for me over the years. I try to focus on the good times like our trip to Disney World when I was 8 or 10 or whatever. Things like that make me smile. It reminds me that you do care about your children. You're not a bad person. You just need to see the light.

Maybe one day we'll see each other again.

Sincerely,

Bryan *Michael* Hrablicht

(Author's note: Bryan's italics on *Michael*, not mine.)

41

Bryan's Birthday Phone Call to Dad

I knew something was coming after Bryan's midnight phone call to David on his birthday. Every year, David waits for the Happy Birthday calls from his kids. Many times, over the years, nothing. (Don't even get me started on the Merry Christmas calls that never come. And on Father's Day, David gets a card signed with paw prints from *our* lovable furry critters, not to be confused with the grubby paws of *his* loathsome critters who don't send cards.) Sometimes the birthday calls would come the next day. Sometimes he would call them. But it was never a *happy* birthday when they talked. Even Pizza Boy, who got into the habit of sending a birthday card once in a while and calling regularly, would somehow drop a bomb of information about the latest problems with Bucky, Bryan or Cindy. Yeah, Happy Birthday Dad! Have a great day!

So the night before Bryan's email arrived, the phone call came. Actually, it came at 12:35 a.m., so it was technically the day after David's birthday. We were already in bed. It was Bryan. As the conversation got longer, David walked farther and farther away from our bedroom and finally into the garage. I guess he didn't want to bother me with his end of the conversation. But later he told me that Bryan was blaming him for all of his problems again, specifically because we moved to Florida. Well, finally something new! We never heard that before.

I guess it didn't matter that we waited until he graduated from high school and told him he should come with us and go to college in Florida to get away from his dysfunctional siblings and co-dependent mother. And I guess it didn't matter that we often took him to Florida over the years so he could get used to the idea. I guess it didn't matter that I spent lots of time and energy on that University of Florida trip with him, trying to convince him to stay with us. None of that mattered. On this night, or rather, early morning, he told David his main problems started when we moved to Florida. Well, he might be right at that. (That's if you don't count the drinking, pot smoking, lying and FBI arrest as problems when we were still in Connecticut.) Unfortunately, Bryan was placing the blame too far south. David and I provided him with an escape. Instead, he chose to stay in his chaotic comfort zone and become one of the co-dependents he so often criticized when he was a little kid. Why did he join their ranks? Was it because we didn't approve of them and he wanted to rebel against us? Couldn't be. He knew society in general did not approve of their behavior? What was it about their lifestyle that attracted him? It must have been something, because he decided to stay with them.

Anyway, according to Bryan, his big problems started when we moved to Florida and that's the main thing David took away from that phone call, more guilt. Happy Birthday Dad!

A little after 1 a.m., they hung up. Then David called Jack to report on Bryan's rants and get his perspective. That phone conversation lasted about a half-hour with David pacing and ending up in the garage again. I went to sleep. I knew I'd get a detailed report first thing in the morning.

David and I have no secrets from each other, not even our email passwords. He's welcome to view mine and I can get into his. We rarely do. However, this time I was diligently on the lookout for something from Bryan. I'm so glad I found it and deleted it from his email before it ruined the day after his birthday too. But I forwarded it to myself so I could show David later. After I read it, I figured I'd just wait a week or so for David's current somber mood to change. Undoubtedly this email was going to set him back again, but I couldn't keep it from him forever. Bryan was bound to follow up somehow and I wanted David to be forewarned. So my plan was to wait a week. I figured it would take Bryan at least that long to either sober up or follow up. But first, I consulted Julie. I knew she had already been through this, as always.

Julie,

Attached is an email that came to David from Bryan today. I deleted it. I'll show it to him eventually, but right now I think he needs a break. What do you think?

And who the hell is *Michael*? Bryan's middle name is *David*.

Kerry

Hey Ker,

Unfuckingbelievable! I read some of it to Kevin. He then showed me an email from his ex-wife, who changed her home phone number and asked Kevin not togive it to his girls if they ever call again. They both owe her money and then yell at her and cut her off, thinking that excuses the debt.

Trisha, who is 49, owes her $400 on a gas credit card! Don't you just want to beat the shit out of them sometimes!! I think I would feel better!!

Michael?

Good luck.

Julie

In the meantime, I tried to find out if there was any truth behind Bryan's rant. There wasn't.

First of all, this "living a healthier lifestyle" shit was just that. Shit. This email was written at 7 a.m. He was on the phone with David at 12:35 a.m. Then I checked his Facebook page. He was on it at 2:37 a.m., posting a video from a movie about a kid who kills his parents. Isn't that special? He went back to his Facebook page at 4:24 a.m. to post a comment about the movie:

> *"It's one of the finest...a smart child outwits his parents because they neglect him...simply beautiful."*

Neglected! I'll show him neglected.

Anyway, the most consecutive hours of sleep he could have gotten was two and a half. So much for a healthier lifestyle. So much for the truth.

As for his pothead brother, Bryan's rant was merely another one of those drunken outrageous exaggerations. There are a few threads of truth to the pot smoking and the nighttime schedule, but hey, he delivers pizzas. No one eats them for breakfast. I've talked to him at all hours of the day and he sounds fine to me. And the painkillers are ibuprofen and he doesn't abuse them. He's been at our house for a couple of weeks every now and then. Even David would notice behavior like Bryan was reporting. Besides, ever since Jack became a diabetic a few years ago, he seems to be on top of his health issues. What Bryan remembers as Jack "drinking himself to death" was actually the pivotal point of the diabetes diagnosis and had nothing to do with alcohol. The "wheelchair" bit Bryan wrote about had to do with the early days of his diabetes when he was terribly underweight and weak. And the "synthetic heroin?" Well, we're all still wondering about that one. No evidence or mention of it before or since.

But all around, none of them are pictures of health. I swear, Bucky, Pizza Boy, Cindy and Bryan could put out more than a nicotine factory in exhaled cigarette smoke. Makes me feel bad about all those non-smoking, law-abiding, altruistic, employed, tax-paying citizens with no arrest records who are suffering with cancer. It's just not fair.

The grocery expense? Wonder where he came up with that one? Bryan has never spent his own hard-earned money on groceries because he hasn't earned any. Was he learning to pinch pennies with food stamps? I knew that part of the email would kill my Republican husband who spews constantly about "the goddamned Democratic Socialized Society that goddamned Obama is creating." Well jeez, if it wasn't for our dear President, David might have to fork over another $400 a month to keep both boys smoking, drinking and eating Elio's pizza.

Those court appearances he mentioned were from the Memorial Day weekend escapade when a drunken Bryan tried to kill his drunken sister. Although from the reports we got from Jack and Cindy (drunken reports from her, sober or pot-tinged from him), it seems that the only charges that might have been pursued were the ones by the police officers. Bucky somehow got Cindy to dismiss her complaint against Bryan. And now that Bryan is living in the same apartment with both of them, well, you can see why Cindy probably needs a good stiff drink every now and then. I know I would.

The student loan was the big surprise in David's birthday email from Bryan. David eventually called Jack to confirm the loan. Yes, they took it out, despite the fact that Bryan wasn't actually going to school at the time. They got $4,800. Ah, the social services for the young and needy. Dontcha just love this country? Even Bryan admitted in his email that he was using it for cigarettes and car repairs.

There was so much drunken rage in this letter from Bryan that I knew it needed a response. I love a writing challenge and I knew any response had to be written so that it could be read over and over again. I only hoped it would be read someday by someone who was sober. I wrote it and sent it at the end of August and as far as I can tell (it's December as I write this), it hasn't been read by a sober person yet. Maybe some day, but not this day or any day in the near future. We're still on the downhill part of this roller coaster ride and picking up speed. We always pick up speed around the holidays.

And as for "Michael," Jack clued us in. It seems that Bryan identifies with the character of Michael Corleone from *The Godfather.* Hmm. Michael Corleone killed his brother Fredo and brother-in-law Carlo. He didn't have a problem with his sister Connie. He was very respectful to his parents. And he wasn't a drunk. He even went to church. He also had a job, a big important job. I wonder what part of the character Bryan *Michael* Hrablicht actually identifies with? Or maybe he's mixing up Michael with Sonny, the impulsive and violent Corleone brother.

42

Dear Fucking Bryan

Dear Bryan,

Remember when we once discussed co-dependency? I'm not sure you will because you were not sober at the time, but the point I tried to make with you is about how crippling it is. I used the example of your mother and sister. I told you how Cindy needs to be around her mother because, in her deteriorating condition from her alcoholism, she feels superior to her. And your mother keeps Cindy around because she feels superior to her also. Look at what your mother's life has become. It's like going out to a social event with an ugly friend: You know you are going to be perceived as the pretty one in comparison to the piece of shit you drag along with you. Cindy is her shit. And your mom is Cindy's shit. That's what keeps those two together. That's how you were with Jack. And don't you feel superior to your mother and sister? In fact, by the tone of your email, you seem to feel superior to everyone.

Your mother is now *your* co-dependent. She needs to feel needed, no matter how bad the situation is. She's not doing what's best for you. She's doing what's best for her. If she had thrown Cindy out years ago, Cindy might have straightened out. If you are allowed to hit rock bottom, you will find the strength to work your way out of the gutter. No food, no shelter, no toilet paper. There's nowhere to go but up from there. Your mother would be better off and so would Cindy if she left Cindy to fend for herself many years ago. I remember your grandmother telling your mother this, but unfortunately she didn't listen.

Despite what you call the "peace" of your current environment, you're getting sucked into a situation that will only spiral downward. Your "peace" is just complacency. You don't have to do anything as long as you're there for your needy mother, and you think you're okay because you get to watch people you feel are beneath you. At age 24, you should be out on your own, not living with mommy. She shouldn't be taking anything from you and you shouldn't be taking anything from her. Take a sober look at your brother and sister. You might as well be looking in a mirror. That is you right now too. Why are you letting this happen?

You don't have the kind of mother who ever loved her children for themselves, only for what they could get for her. For you, she got a check for $25,000. We have a copy of the bill of sale, so she can't deny this. She's not very bright. We would have paid more to get you out of her toxic environment. But a lot of people have bad parents and still go on to exciting, productive lives. You never hear about Charles Manson's kids getting into trouble. *(An extreme example, I know. But it's true.)* It's unfortunate that you don't need some kind of license to become a parent. Neither of yours is in danger of being surprised by the Parent of the Year prize patrol. Hey, neither were mine.

We've all seen the way your mother uses Cindy. She needed a friend after the divorce and used Cindy to smoke and drink with her and to upset your father with her accusations of molestation. Your mother needed to feel superior to your father too and that's how she did it. Of course when Cindy was sober, she always apologized to your dad for letting her mother put her up to that. Perhaps if someone had offered your mother $25,000 for her daughter, she might have taken it and moved on with her life. But no one did. She created the monster and I guess everybody felt she should deal with her. Nobody wanted Cindy after your mother got through molding her in her own image. Just ask your aunts. Why didn't anyone in your mother's family help? Because they didn't want to. I remember your father and me discussing it. Neither of us ever wanted Cindy around. The reason was that we didn't want her near you.

Your mother neglected both you and Jack in favor of Cindy except to use you as conduits to your father. And if you feel that she wants you now, I ask you to think about why. What will it get her? You can bet she's thought about it. You might ask her about that $450 she owes your father for helping her with the car a few weeks ago. She used Cindy for that. What is she going to use you for? I don't hate your mother. Why waste the energy? I hardly know her, but I do know what she's done over the past 17 years. She's a pitiful excuse for a mother, a stereotypical needy woman. I know how she neglected you. I know how much money she went through with nothing to show for it. No home, no education, nothing special for you kids and not much of a future. I still laugh hysterically when I think about the time she invited your father to lunch to ask him to buy her a house. Unfuckingbelievable. How can a person exist with such a lack of pride and self esteem? Bryan, everything I predict is from experience, not emotion. I know what she's done and she's very predictable. In fact, all of you are, just like her.

I could have written the email you sent to your father and just mixed up the names. Not one of you is better than the other, although each of you thinks you are and that's what sustains you and keeps you living like white trash.

I've known a lot over the years. Most of which I've shared with your father even when he didn't want to hear it. But there are some things I just let him find out for himself. Fast forward to today and just let me assure you his blinders are off regarding all of you. He speaks in ways I've never heard before and I'm loving it. We have a wonderful life these days. We go to the gym and pool together. We go out to dinner often. He's even made some new male friends and he does some dinners with them when I'm out with the ladies. He's getting healthier as he closes the door on all of you and it can't be fast enough for me. He says he'll never go back to Connecticut. You may not think he's as smart as you are but he's smart enough to know it wouldn't do anybody any good, especially him.

He and I have talked about what the future is probably going to be for all of you. You're all likely to die in very sad ways and I think he's prepared for that now. We just hope there are no innocent lives involved. We constantly fear a drunken car crash where the drunk survives but kills an innocent family. I think that would be your dad's "rock bottom." What's yours? I guess it's got to be worse than being in jail and putting your sister in the hospital.

Do you have anything in your life to be proud of? Does the rest of your family? Really. What have you done to help people or make the world a better place? You've been nothing but a user. A welfare case. Look at what other people your age are doing. Have you fallen too far behind to ever dig yourself out of your hole?

If you re-read the email you sent to your dad when you're sober, use your education in creative writing to see that your main character sees himself as a do-gooder, savior and victim all at once. It's a clear sign of narcissism. Of course it's understandable in your current condition when you've chosen to surround yourself with drunks, druggies and co-dependents. If you ever see clearly again, perhaps you'll make better choices and get away from the cancer.

Run, don't walk. Only you can save yourself and you have to do it by yourself. All by yourself. The *family* dynamics in your current situation will kill you. You'd be better off on the streets or in a shelter with people who won't use you and perhaps will challenge you to do something good for yourself or for others. I hope you see the light and find your way out. But we will not help you. We're done. A real man makes his own way in the world despite what has happened in his past. You are "on the brink of disaster" and you need to make "great changes." You keep going backwards. Don't you see that? Are you afraid of failure? Afraid of success? Independent productive people have lots of both once they get off their asses and off welfare.

I'd advise you to get a job doing manual labor. Tire yourself out while you're earning a paycheck. It will make a big difference in your life and you will be able to see evidence of progress every day. It'll open up a whole new world to you and maybe you'll find a way out of the mess you've put yourself back into. If not, you're going to die there and it will probably be soon.

I hope you find the strength to get out.

Sincerely,

Kerry

After Bryan received this email, he forwarded it to his father and asked if David knew I sent it. By that time, I had shown Bryan's original email to David and we had discussed how we were losing the never-ending battle for truth and sobriety. So to answer Bryan's question of whether David knew about my email, he got a one-word reply: *Yes.*

43

Happy 32ⁿᵈ Birthday to Cindy

It really doesn't matter that I specifically call this chapter "Happy 32ⁿᵈ." You see, the same thing happens on every one of Cindy's birthdays with only a few minor details changed. Really, it's like a *Twilight Zone* episode, the old sci-fi t.v. show, not the new vampire movies. On the other hand, an unscrupulous blood-sucker is not a bad way to describe Cindy. No wait, it's more like that movie *Groundhog Day* where Bill Murray goes through the same thing every day until he realizes he must change from within and become a better person if he's ever going to get on with his life. But which one of us is Bill Murray?

It's not me. I don't do the same thing over and over with regard to Cindy. I'm always willing to step it up and challenge her to feed and clothe herself and wipe her own ass.

Cindy can't be Bill Murray because he eventually *gets it*. Her brain is so pickled from the alcohol by now that I don't think she has the potential to get anything except the same old thing from her mother (tolerance or indifference) and father (cash and hope).

So David must be Bill Murray. He lives every one of her birthdays in the same way, expecting the passing of another year to bring about a difference in her. Why? It's been at least 16 drunken years now and nothing has changed. There has been no catalyst in her life. Hello! Catalyst job open! Parent-like person please apply.

Every year I ask David why he thinks her mother puts up with her. He usually says it's because her mother loves her and only her. But not this year. This year he said he thinks it's because Bucky is afraid of her. Cindy has become a very large, fat woman who is drunk and out-of-control most of the time. Her mother carries a few extra pounds but is twice as old as Cindy. Bucky also has a job, so Cindy is left on her own in the apartment all day long. That's plenty of time for her to wreak havoc on her mom's things.

As for the details of this year, they're just bigger and better than in years past. After all was said and done, Cindy ended up being taken to the drunk tank by the local police, and after the initial phone call and subsequent phone messages, we had a pretty peaceful day.

A couple of weeks before the big day, Pizza Boy told David that Cindy can't get her car fixed because she doesn't have the money. She hasn't worked in almost three years, but she always seems to have money for booze and cigarettes. Either mom is footing the bill or she could still be on unemployment. Thank you for that extension, President Obama. So David bought a birthday card and put a $300 check in it. He said it's for her birthday and Christmas, so she can get her car fixed. He normally would have sent her just $50 for each occasion.

Okay, by now I should know better than to comment on the gift. (Oh no, maybe I am Bill Murray! Yikes!) I told David it was probably a bad idea to send a check to an alcoholic. Then he started to argue with me about how she needed the money to get her car fixed. I calmly told him that it probably wasn't a good idea for a drunk to have a working car either. So he asked, "What should I have done?" Mistake on my part, but I answered, " Send her a sweater, asshole." Perhaps I should have stopped at sweater, but I didn't.

You see, these are the little arguments that make our life together less-than-joyous, but exciting. And they always involve the kids. I know I could shut my mouth and just let him send the money. But, silly me, I want him to think about the consequences. If she ends up killing someone on the road, I don't think David will ever be the same, and he's not so great now. But the give-and-take between us isn't that bad anymore. The aftermath of these little discussions is a breeze too. We look at each other as if to say, "Okay, I hear you, but let's just drop it." And life goes on. Comfort in repetition.

So on her big day in November, she called in the morning, already drunk. However, David didn't know this for awhile because he kept talking after he picked up the phone. He kept going on about the weather, her birthday, the check he sent, the car, etc. He didn't let her get a word in edgewise until he was out of breath. Then she started her drunken rage about how he ruined her life. Praise be to God, he actually hung up.

When she called back, he told me not to answer the phone. Sometimes, he gets it. I set a specific ring tone for her number so we'd always be alerted to her calls. She left a glorious message when we didn't answer. First it was directed at me, "the evil bitch that her father married." And then she let loose on Daddy, "the child molester who ruined my life because of what he did to me." *Groundhog Day* all over again.

Now let me take a moment to remind you I didn't even meet David until after he was divorced. So this "evil bitch" had nothing to do with stealing David. And it was Bucky who wanted out of that union. It was also Bucky who told Cindy they could get more money if Cindy would accuse her father of molesting her. And it was always Cindy who apologized for that when she was sober, because she knows he didn't do anything to her and she just said it "so mom could get more money from you." The molestation rants got bigger and better as the years went on. This year, Cindy also said that Bryan told her he was sodomized by his father. Of course Bryan never actually said this drunk or sober, but I guess even Cindy gets bored with the same old story year after year.

I listened to the message first and then I gave the phone to David. I told him the next time he wants to spend $300 on booze, he should think about stocking our bar before he wrote out any checks. Know what he did next? He blamed me for *making him* listen to the message. Yep, thank God for Dr. Perera's words ringing in my ears, telling me to let David clean up his own mess. I said something like, "Forget you." Yeah, that's what I remember saying.

I pointed out to him that I wasn't upset, even though most of her rant was directed at me this time. I understood that she was always going to be like this and it didn't matter what I did. She was always going to hate me and blame everyone else for her problems. It also didn't matter what he did or how much money he gave her, she was always going to resent him and want more. She thinks she's entitled. Her mother made her that way and apparently, there's no going back. The sooner he understands this and dismisses her behavior without so much emotion, the better off he'll be. Detach and be free I say!

One interesting fact about this call was that she used some of the phrases I had written in my response to Bryan after his drunken email to David on David's birthday. I could tell because she doesn't have the vocabulary to use a word like *narcissist* on her own. Maybe that's what fueled her rant this time, reading about herself from my point of view.

So all this happened on the morning of her birthday. By early evening, Pizza Boy called to tell us the rest of the story. She was so loud and belligerent throughout the day that one of the neighbors called the police. They came and took her away to the drunk tank again. The next day, she was back home with mommy as though nothing had ever happened. No consequences. Ever.

I'm sure there are other families dealing with this problem and it's too bad that the family member with the brain, if there is one, is helpless. You can't make a so-called consenting adult do anything without their consent. The only way people like this are ever going to get any help to change is if they kill someone, or do something almost as bad, so that they remain in custody. Then the law and social services will take over. It's a morbid waiting game. You're waiting for someone to die. The only question is: Will it be an innocent bystander or your drunken family member?

I heard a report on the radio recently that it takes $55,000 to house one prisoner in California. Yet it takes only $50,000 a year for a person to attend Stanford University. That's sad. I know the answer is not to send our prisoners to Stanford. And even if we did, would they achieve like other Stanford Alumni (Condoleezza Rice, Jim Plunkett, Sally Ride, Tom Watson, Eunice Kennedy Shriver)? Why are we spending money like that on people like Cindy? Yes, I know there are rapists and murderers in prison in California and she's not as bad as one of them. But I've got to believe there are also prisoners who have committed vehicular homicide or manslaughter, in a drunken rage or by accident. She *is* capable of that. She's destined for it.

If the enabling ends only when she does something worse than her family can handle, what good will that do? Why can't the enabling end now, before someone gets hurt? I can't answer that. I survive in the midst of all this because, although I have no control over it, I won't let it control me.

So every November, all I can say is, "Happy Friggin' Birthday Cindy." Here we go again.

44

THAT Would Kill You?

This morning I got a message on Facebook from one of my former students, Andrew Beck. He's in the graduate program for film at New York University and part of a small group that just won a big grant from the San Antonio Film Commission. This fall, they'll be producing their film in San Antonio with that grant money.

So after spreading the word to my other former students and the world on Facebook, I told David. He was less-than-thrilled, as usual, about a major achievement by a college student who wasn't his kid.

> David: That's good. What's that other guy doing? Your favorite student. The one in California.

> Kerry: That's Adam Bagger. He's directing commercials and other things out in L.A. and he's writing a screenplay.

> David: He's the one who's AC/DC, right? *(AC/DC is David's euphemism for homosexual.)*

> Kerry: No, Adam is living with a beautiful blonde woman who works in health care. They just got engaged.

David: Oh, who's the one who's AC/DC?

Kerry: That's Candace.

David: Candace? That pretty girl? She's a lesbian? The one who's father played for the Dallas Cowboys?

Kerry: Yep, that Candace.

David: Oh no, that poor guy. Wonder what he thinks of that. That would kill me!

Kerry: THAT would kill you???? You've got to be kidding. THAT would kill you????

David: Shut up.

45

I'm Not Like *Those* People

---

*"When I came to recovery, I realized that being a child for
28 years nearly killed me."*

— Author unknown

That's my favorite saying from a long list of quotes I've read by
people involved in 12-step programs. I see the truth in it every
day. Adults who are treated as children don't learn survival skills.

After Bryan had to be removed from our house by a sheriff,
and David nearly had a stroke in the weeks that followed, I decided it
was time to drag my husband to Al-Anon meetings. Yes, drag. And
yes, kicking and screaming. I even had to promise him we'd stop for ice
cream after the first meeting.

I thought the people we met at the meetings were wonderful
for being able to share what they had learned over the years. I was
especially grateful to the men and women who were there because of
their alcoholic adult children. Their stories were similar to ours, except
that they were actively trying to heal and move on with their own
lives, away from the alcoholics. They weren't always successful, and
they shared those hard lessons too. I was thrilled. We were finally

among experienced parents of alcoholics who were trying to do the right thing for themselves and their children. These were my kind of people. I had hope, until I asked David what he thought about these meetings.

He said, "I'm not like *those* people." Funny, that's the same thing Bryan said about being housed at that in-patient facility he hated so much. I think they both find it hard to live surrounded by so many mirrors, but that's just my opinion.

Anyway, I stopped dragging David to meetings. He wasn't ready. He hadn't hit rock bottom yet.

I had been to a few Al-Anon meetings in Connecticut years before I met David. I went to get help in understanding my parents. I was searching for a way to help them. Al-Anon taught me I couldn't help them. I could only help myself. That was a big breakthrough for me. Thank God I was ready to hear it. I spent my childhood trying to take control because my parents were out of control and now I was understanding that control of someone else was out of my reach. This lesson needs refreshing. That bears repeating. *This lesson needs refreshing.* It's so easy to slip back into a caretaker role when someone you love looks like they need mothering.

After my own mother died from cirrhosis of the liver, I felt guilty for not being able to save her. So I tried to save someone else.

I started dating a second-generation alcoholic. Bill's father drank himself to death and Bill seemed to blame his mother's early death, years later, on the tough years his father put her through. I did everything for him that I thought I should have done for my mother. I threatened him, begged him, and cajoled him to stop drinking. And he did, most of the time. I also dragged him to counseling. But what I learned, again, was that *our* problem was not *my* problem. It was *his*. We had two big break-ups over three years before I finally saw the light, wished him well, and moved on.

On my first date with David, we talked about addictions. It was very important for both of us to move forward in our lives without being touched by alcoholism. His situation almost mirrored mine. His father was an alcoholic and his mother started drinking to keep up with him. He had the same memories of family fights fueled by alcohol and never wanted to go through that again. Both his parents were dead and he was an only child. My father was still living and finally not drinking. My brother and I never seemed to have any addictions. It appeared that, although David and I came through the storm scarred, it gave us the strength to be honest with each other about our intolerance of addicts.

Over that first dinner he told me about his college basketball and baseball years and how he was the only one on the teams who didn't drink or smoke pot. Back in the early 1960s that was probably looked upon as weird, but David was determined to stay in control. Besides, he was a scholar-athlete and a star. If he said "no," there wasn't any peer pressure because the other kids looked up to him. I'm sure he'd like to think his refusal to get high helped other less-disciplined kids opt out also.

Our 15-year age difference put me in college over a decade later, but in more or less the same kind of environment from high school on. I was one of the "smart kids" and I filled my time with plenty of activities and lots of studying. I also had a job doing on-air radio news at age 16. I'm not sure what my classmates thought about my ability to stay sober or my absence at parties. No one really questioned it or even tempted me with anything. I'm sorry to say they probably thought that I considered myself above them when it came to maturity and intellect. That wasn't so. I was afraid to let anyone get too close. I felt bad that I didn't have a lot of friends. But keeping my distance kept me out of trouble and kept my alcoholic home life a secret. Back in the '70s, we didn't share.

In the more than 30 years since, I've renewed a lot of high school acquaintances and count them among my very good friends. And now we share. We take pride in what we did to survive and we take comfort in the fact that we're still here when many of our classmates are not. We also have new problems and are able to share some of those. I even have friends who tell me they have had difficulties with stepchildren. Of course their difficulties don't include multiple detoxes (detoxi?), an F.B.I. arrest and attempted sororicide, but I'm sure they think they've got problems.

Whenever I go home to Connecticut to visit my dad and my hairdresser, I always contact as many of my high school classmates as possible to join me for a night out at a local bar or restaurant. Some drink beer and some drink Coke. Some are currently on a step and some have finished all 12. Others have never been touched by addiction. But nobody, absolutely nobody, challenges anyone to do shots. You do better when you know better.

46

Good Morning Email

Dear Kerry,

Good morning! I thought I'd start your day with the latest from one of Kevin's princesses.

Last week, Terry (who is over 40 years old) texted her father that he ought to read some books about parenting but she didn't include any suggested titles. A little late, dontcha think? Anyway, this morning, she texted Kevin about only having $9 in her checking account and needing Zyrtec medicine. Kevin texted her back that she'll do just as well on a generic. I was proud of him.

So after she gets the text about using the generic medicine, she asks if he has read any of the parenting books. He said, "No, you didn't send the titles."

She comes back with, "I'm thru with all 3 of you."

He responds, "Me, Julie and who else?"

She answers, "You, mom and Trisha. Julie was never a part of it."

He didn't respond.

Her next text was in all caps, "FUCK YOU."

And how is your morning going?

Julie

Dear Julie,

No chaos here yet, but it's early. And why don't you re-read your email to see the really good news.

You did it! You successfully extricated yourself from the shit. Hey, you were "never a part of it." That's as close to a compliment or a thank you as you're ever gonna get. High five girlfriend!

Parenting books. Hmm. Why didn't I think of that. I always gave David books like *Boundaries* and other co-dependency titles I picked up at Al-Anon. What was I thinking? I should have started with Dr. Spock and worked my way up to Dr. Kevorkian.

Hope the rest of your day gets better.

Kerry

47

And So This Is Christmas

And so this is Christmas
And what have we done?
Another year over.
A new one just begun.

John Lennon wrote the song, *And So This Is Christmas,* about the end of war. The first part of that song always pops into my head at the start of the war-like hijinx of the holiday season among the three imbeciles and the Mother-of-the-Year. It usually begins on Christmas Eve with a drunken phone call from Cindy, or a report on Cindy's state of drunkenness from Pizza Boy. But this year, whoa, it began on December 20 at 4:30 p.m., which led me to believe I already had Julie beat in the race for the Christmas crown. Or at least I had the early lead. The last I heard, she and Kevin were still enjoying the I'm-not-talking-to-my-father resolution of the remaining two girls who were now in their late 40s. And their mother never gave them her new phone number, so she was enjoying the severed ties too.

We were planning to go out to an early dinner with my father, who was visiting from Connecticut. Logan's Roadhouse or TGI Friday's in the Orlando tourist area are usually good places to take him. He enjoys the 45-minute ride and the typical American menu. David loves both places because they always have coupons or specials so he can get his money's worth. We planned on leaving home at 4:45 p.m.

At 4:30 p.m., Bryan called and kept David on the phone nearly an hour. Never a good sign. Earlier in the day, David had to call Pizza Boy to ask him to call Bryan and tell Bryan to call David. For some reason, David's calls to Bryan at his mother's apartment did not go through and David didn't know why. Pizza Boy clued him in. Bucky blocks calls. Pizza Boy knew this because she had once blocked *his* calls. She told him she blocked David's calls because "he upsets Cindy and Bryan." How, by sending them money? By listening to their drunken rants? By bailing them out of jail or paying for rehab or school or...? How in the world had David upset *them*? So armed with this new knowledge of call-blocking, David was upset about that, as well as not hearing from Bryan about any upcoming tuition for the January semester.

David had been going over our income tax figures earlier in the day and wanted to know if he'd be spending any more tuition money for Bryan. The expense, if paid in this calendar year, would add to our itemized deductions and get us a nifty refund of about $400.

David explained this to Bryan over the phone. Then there was a pause and I heard him say, "Bryan, I can't believe you said that to me. I can't believe you said that."

Bryan was mad at him for wanting to take the deduction and David really couldn't believe it. Neither could I. What difference did it make to Bryan if David got a deduction? It would actually benefit Bryan by giving David more money to send to him when he needed to buy booze and cigarettes.

Could Bryan be upset that his father wanted the refund in lieu of it being absorbed into government programs, like food stamps and student loans? Bryan and Pizza Boy actually applied for and got those. Or maybe this was a political statement. Geez, that's all David needs on top of the drugs, alcohol and violence: a Democrat.

David always said he'd never tolerate drug use, smoking and excessive drinking by his kids, even though that's exactly what he does. Tolerate? Hell, he donates to the cause.

And don't get me started on the time Bryan dated an African American girl, which I'm sure he did just to be able to send photos of the two of them together to his multi-culturally-unaware father. After I found out about this girl, I waited for David to tell me about her. It's seven years later and I'm still waiting. But as for politics, I think he just assumed his kids would be Republicans without having to warn them of the dangers proliferated by the Democratic Party. Well, you know what happens when you assume (ass-u-me).

From what I could tell, Bryan was accusing David of *only* wanting to pay the tuition in order to get the deduction. I realize a drunk sociopath who doesn't work and receives food stamps probably doesn't understand this whole deduction thing. But really, it's not like David would be getting more money back than he was spending. It's basic math. Surely I thought, even Bryan must realize this. I guess it's more likely that he just didn't care. This was something to rant about, and he was probably drunk. After all, it was after 4:30 p.m. He and his sister (the one he tried to kill on Memorial Day weekend, just seven months ago, but with whom he was now living "in peace" at their mother's 2-bedroom apartment) probably had a few cocktails by now.

The conversation continued. David tried to explain that he wanted a deduction *if* he could get one, rather than just paying the tuition in the next calendar year and *not* getting a deduction. He repeated this to Bryan over and over and over, calmly explaining the math of it all. It's this repetition that confirmed to me that Bryan was drunk. Even he would have ended this call if he were sober.

David finally got tired of repeating himself, telling Bryan, "I don't have to pay the tuition at all. How would you like that?" I wish I could have heard Bryan's answer. We're going on year number eight for this liberal arts college education which has been interrupted by blackouts, detox, re-tox, time to find himself, jail, another detox, another re-tox, rehab, court appearances and more. The only thing it hasn't been interrupted by is work. Nope, not even a pizza-delivery job. I guess his older brother isn't an inspiration to him either.

I often wonder why David stays on the phone so long, regurgitating the same common sense to Bryan and Cindy. Is he waiting for them to sober up? I swear, he gives them enough time. But what they're probably doing is drinking more while he's talking. What else are they going to do? It's not like they need to multi-task while on the phone. They're not even solo-tasking when they're off the phone. They've got nothing to do. Yet David can't seem to hang up. Maybe he's addicted to the chaos and stupidity of the situation. He couldn't possibly think he's doing them any good over the phone, could he?

The phone call with Bryan ended around 5:30 p.m. and by then David didn't want to go "way out there" for dinner, even though earlier he told me he had another coupon for Logan's so we could have saved money. We pinch pennies, but I'm sure Bryan and Cindy are drinking top-shelf booze. Hell, just recently David attempted to bar me from *eating* off the top shelf. He actually tried to take away my General Mills Multi-Grain Cheerios. Damn him.

Every morning I have a small bowl of Multi-Grain Cheerios. I eat it dry, with a large mug of tea with milk. No sugar. I'm sweet enough. David doesn't get up until after 11 a.m. and shuns any kind of breakfast food. However, in order to take his many pills and supplements, he likes to have something in his stomach. Just this month, he's started to eat a small bowl of my Cheerios with milk. Since he's become familiar with the box, I felt safe in adding Multi-Grain Cheerios to a small shopping list he was going out for by himself. I don't know what it is about multi-grains, but that's the variety of Cheerios that's the most expensive. It's $3.48 for a 16.2 ounce box at Walmart.

David can't handle the vastness of Walmart alone, so he shops at Publix, where I'm sure my Cheerios cost a little more. Well lo and behold, it wasn't even an issue to pick out the multi-grains rather than some other kind of cheaper Cheerios, because he found what he calls "the Publix brand of *your* Cheerios." You would have thought he struck gold by the way he excitedly told me "this 12.25 ounce box of Honey Oats (notice the absence of the term multi-grain) only cost $1.49."

I said, "Good for you (quoting Dr. Perera whenever I can). Where's my Multi-Grain Cheerios?"

"This is better," he said, despite never having put even one of those Honey Oats into his mouth. He bought two boxes on the price alone.

"Better for whom?" I said. "I like my Multi-Grain Cheerios."

"But this costs less than half of what yours costs," he answered. "And it's the *same* thing."

He might be right, although I doubt it. There was no mention of multi-grains on this Publix cereal box of Honey Oats, and he doesn't have much of a track record in the I-was-right department. But I wasn't about to debate the advertising and marketing costs of General Mills products versus a store brand, or take a taste test. I just filed this episode away, knowing it would come in handy someday to make a point about us saving money here in Florida in order to be able to buy Cindy and Bryan more liquor in Connecticut. Hence, my Multi-Grain Cheerios troubles are now validated on these pages.

As for dinner, we went to the restaurant here in our little village, only a five-minute golf cart ride away. We ran into neighbors in the parking lot, and thankfully, all seven of us sat together. Otherwise, it would have been a very tense meal. David was in one of his post-phone-call moods. This time it surfaced as non-stop talking. I think he can't stop taking control of situations in *our* life, because he relinquishes so much control to the drunks in *his* life. It was a long dinner. Service was slow. The others at the table didn't want dessert. Neither did I, but I ordered it for me and my dad anyway, just to pad the bill a little. After all, David is saving a ton of money by buying Honey Oats for himself now. I thought I'd spend a little of it before he has to haul all that cash to the bank.

After dinner, we found that the Tennessee vs. Stanford women's college basketball game was on t.v. Two of the top five teams in the nation. It's a game that all three of us wanted to watch, even though the west coast starting time made it a late 10 p.m. game for us. It was a great first half. We took the required bathroom breaks, got some snacks and sat down to watch the second half. Well, my dad and I did anyway.

The phone rang at halftime and Bryan's name and number came up on the television screen. I love that great warning service that comes with our cable t.v. package. But despite the warning and the time, after 11 p.m., David answered the phone. It was Cindy. She's always drunk by this hour, so I figured David would hang up and come back to the game in minutes, if not sooner. Nope. He stayed on the phone with her past the seven-minute mark in the game. (That's over a half-hour for you non-sports fans.) Twice, I tried to get him off the phone by telling him he was missing the game. Each time, he waved me off. I waved back at him, but thought it best that I didn't actually let him see my hand gesture.

This was almost a repeat of his conversation with Bryan in as much as he kept saying the same things to her over and over and over. I knew she wouldn't even remember the call, so why bother?

Over and over again he tells her, "I'd like to have a relationship with you." Well that's a big fat lie. I'm sure that's the last thing he wants. But she seems to be asking him, over and over, to be available and call her often to give her advice. Advice on what? She doesn't work. She doesn't leave the house except to go to bars. Bryan once told me a local bartender would call him to pick her up when she couldn't walk out on her own. I wonder whom he calls to pick up Bryan. And even if she did ask for, and receive good advice, what would make her take it? She never has before.

After the Memorial Day weekend fiasco in which Bryan put her in the hospital, I advised her to go to a woman's shelter and reach out to the female police officer she met at the hospital. I thought that was great advice. Get out of the toxic environment of living with her mother and homicidal brother and get help. She didn't take that advice. What kind of advice was she looking for? Besides, her mother was going to have to unblock our phone number from their phone if she wanted David to call her at all.

I could tell she also asked David to come back to Connecticut to visit. He hasn't seen her in the eight years since we moved to Florida.

We've met several new people in our neighborhood recently. When they ask how long we've been here, David proudly says, "Eight years and I've never gone back to Connecticut. My wife goes back to see her family, but not me. If people want to see me, they have to come here." He doesn't want to go back. A trip to see his kids is about as far away from his idea of a vacation as you can get. All they bring him is misery. Why would he want to go see them?

Still, he humors her and says, "If we keep talking to each other, maybe this spring I'll come up and visit."

Quite honestly, I'd pay to see that happen if I could actually watch what goes on so I could write about it. On the other hand, I think seeing her and the rest of them at one time would literally kill David. I mean it. Heart attack or stroke or a nasty car accident because he's a terrible driver anyway and worse when he's upset.

So, as the basketball game was winding down on t.v. and she kept him on the phone, I heard him trying to validate his so-called parenting by reciting his recent payouts of Daddy Welfare.

"I sent your mother money ($450) for your car and she said she'd pay me back, but I haven't seen a cent. I sent you $300 for your birthday and Christmas to use for your car too. I've sent Bryan $250 a month for the past couple of months. I've sent, I've sent, I've sent." The Bryan payout was news to me.

None of them ever ask for advice, just money. That's all they ever call him for and that's all he ever gives. It would be the perfect symbiotic relationship if it didn't have such a detrimental effect on all of them. No responsibility. No discipline. No ambition. No gratitude. And for David, serious depression. Just once, I'd like to hear one of them ask for money and have him respond as a parent with a brain, "You'll have your own money if you get a job" or "GET A FUCKING JOB, YOU BLOOD-SUCKING PIECE OF SHIT." Either response would be fine with me.

The basketball game David couldn't wait to watch was almost over. It was time to stop the madness. I called the home phone from my cell phone to give David an out, if he wanted one. I know from experience that this beeping through a call is very annoying, so I kept it ringing. He finally hung up his phone and asked, "Is that you calling me?"

"Yes," I answered, adding, "No shit, Sherlock," under my breath.

The game ended. Stanford beat Tennessee. Dad went to bed. David turned on FOX News and I grabbed my laptop to start writing notes of the day's events.

Vice President Joe Biden was on FOX News and David, as usual, called him "an idiot." I'm not the biggest Joe Biden fan either, but at this moment, even he looked smarter than David. As I sat with my laptop, taking down the notes from the evening chaos, I said, "Oh, Joe Biden isn't such an idiot. I know he's done something right. I'll look it up for you." So I googled "Joe Biden children."

"Here it is. Joe raised successful children," I told David. "He's got three kids, two lawyers and one social worker. Not bad for an idiot."

David responded, "Lawyers are the biggest crooks going." He had nothing to say about the social worker. Perhaps he anticipates more social services in the future for his children. I know I do. Maybe someday one of David's kids will meet one of Joe's kids, in a professional capacity of course, not at a dinner party. I may be wrong, but I'm thinking they travel in different social circles.

I said, "At least the Biden kids are all getting paychecks, paying taxes and not living off their father. They might even be Republicans." Silence and a glare came back at me.

David's unemployed, non-educated, food-stamp-collecting *kids* are 36, 32 and 24 at this writing. And if our illustrious Vice President and his three children were to go up against them on the Biden Idiots vs. Hrablicht Imbeciles version of Family Feud, well, I'm sure even David's money would be on the Idiots. He's no fool. Well, at least not in this case, where money would be at stake. He'd look at the track record of each team and play the odds.

Cindy's call tonight, on December 20, was to set David up for more for Christmas. It happens every year. She got her combination birthday and Christmas check in November for her birthday. Now she's looking for something else because she sees Bryan positioning for more. She hasn't worked in at least three years, maybe more. She must be collecting unemployment or drinking with her mother's money. She always seems to have a never-ending supply of booze, cigarettes and food.

After Bryan went through detox again, following the Memorial Day weekend attempt on Cindy's life, he told David he wouldn't ask him for any money because he was going to "get a job and take care of himself and help his mother and yadda, yadda, yadda." David told me this proudly.

Since then, over the past few months, I've asked him, "Has Bryan asked you for money yet?" He always answers, "No," once again, quite proudly, leading me to believe he was NOT providing any money that was not requested. But as I learned from his conversation with Cindy, he lied to me about this. When I confronted him and accused him of lying, he said, "No I didn't. You asked me if he *asked me* for money. He didn't." Once again, no shit, Sherlock. Why should he ask you for money if you're already sending it to him, asshole. I felt like I was back teaching high school, explaining to a teenager why the dog-ate-my-homework excuse doesn't fly. If you have to lie about something you're doing, it's probably something you shouldn't be doing in the first place.

Every day David mentions something about money and our spending, not on luxury items or vacations, but on things like bread and Multi-Grain Cheerios.

While my father is here visiting for two weeks at Christmas, the grocery bill gets padded with his favorites like ice cream, chocolate chip cookies and deli meat. I made a sandwich for my dad the other day. My 84-year-old dad rarely eats the crust of the bread. As I was making the sandwich, David told me not to even put the meat on bread because "he'll just waste it." Of course he was right. Dad did leave most of the bread. So what! A sandwich is made with two slices of bread. If an 84-year-old man wants to leave the crust, let him. And don't tell him, as David did, that he's wasting bread. And don't give it, as David did, to our overweight dog just so you won't throw it away.

Geez, with Bryan's Daddy Welfare payment of $250 a month I could probably buy bread from an actual bakery instead of the packaged bread aisle at Walmart. I might even have a few dollars left over to invest in the real Multi-Grain Cheerios. And don't get me started on the generic frozen pizzas or the $5 one-topping pizza from Little Caesar's. If I had that extra $250 a month, I'd be able to splurge on two toppings at Little Caesar's and maybe even buy one of those fabulous frozen *supreme* pizzas with multiple toppings from DiGiorno's. Ah, if only.

So to continue the saga of our December 20th evening, David went to bed at 12:30 a.m. and turned on an old movie on t.v. I went to bed about 12:45 a.m. with the dog between us and the cat on the other side of me, my back to David. He started rubbing my back. (Ladies, hold your laughter. We know a back rub is never just a back rub.) Well, the last thing I wanted was to be touched by a man who denied my father a crust of bread in order to buy booze that I'm not even going to see, let alone taste. And besides being angry, I'm peri-menopausal.

"Do it yourself, asshole," I tell him.

So he says, "What can I do?" Does he really not know, I wonder.

I respond, "Cut them off. Don't you see all they want is money? They don't care about you. They only call for money. You need to cut them out of our lives."

Then I calmly say to him, "Bryan and Cindy are going to kill themselves like Kevin's daughter, or they're going to kill someone else on the road, if they don't sober up. And you're one of their biggest problems. You treat them like 3-year-olds. Don't you understand what happens to people who can't do anything for themselves?"

He tells me that I shouldn't be so upset because he tries to keep me out of all the shit that happens. I point out to him that I get involved when it affects his mood and behavior and it *always* affects his mood and behavior. I also point out to him that he is perpetuating the problem and he alone has the power to stop it.

And for the first time in a long time I was so angry that I actually wanted out and I told him so. I recently found out that my old job in Connecticut may be open due to the health issues of the woman who replaced me eight years ago. That wouldn't be such a bad move for me.

David said, "You really want to do that?"

I said, "Well, I'm going to have to make a living. Like I told you before we moved here, I was leaving a great job with great pay for the retirement lifestyle, and the retirement lifestyle is obviously not working out for us. You told me it would be a wonderful life where we could do things together, travel a little bit and do what we want. Hell, I can't even buy the real Cheerios without you yelling at me about money, yet you pay for booze and cigarettes for your kids who aren't kids. I need this shit to end."

Kids who are no longer kids. Reminds me, he did say something to Cindy about how she has to do things for herself because she's 32, but that was in the same breath that he told her he'd come to visit, so he was probably just blowing smoke before writing another Daddy Welfare check.

If I really did get out now, I'd have to go back to work, find a place to live and take care of my dog and two cats. There is no way I'm going to leave Spike, Zeke and Eddie with the fucking Father-of-the-Year. Who knows what would become of them. On the other hand, they spend most of their time sleeping, eating and drinking already. And they don't have jobs. How much damage could David do? Might Spike take up smoking with his canine friends, behind the hedges at the dog park? Could Zeke and Eddie take too many hits of catnip? Probably not. Anyway, it's all too much for me at this point. I rationalize that the energy I'd spend on this life change would just about equal all the energy I'm spending in trying to keep us together amidst the drunken chaos. And right now, I'm 1,300 miles away. I really will be better off if I stay here and keep writing. I think.

One more thing, earlier, when he got off the phone with Bryan, he came over and hugged me. David needs me for support. Sometimes I think he genuinely needs me to kick him in the ass. And that's something I enjoy. Talk about a symbiotic relationship! Yay team!

The rest of Christmas week was uneventful except for David moaning about Jack having nowhere to go for Christmas. Pizza Boy said he'd "never, never, never" go to his mother's house and he felt like he wasn't welcome at any of his other relatives' homes because they no longer welcomed his mother. So David tossed around a couple of "poor Jack" remarks that I ignored.

David called Pizza Boy around 11 a.m. on Christmas Day and left a message. Pizza Boy left a message back around 3 p.m. We went to a neighbor's house for dinner and David was out of reach of both our phones. But just in case, I silenced the ringer on the cell phone and unplugged the wall phone. Hey Bucky, I can block too!

That night I asked David if he had ever talked to Jack. He said yes, he called him back. I asked if Jack went anywhere for Christmas.

He said he went to his mother's house. I knew he would. He's co-dependent on the chaos, no different than the other two. Neither Bryan nor Cindy called and David said he didn't expect them to because " the checks were already in the mail."

And this is where I want to say the four of them either lived happily ever far after away from us, or imploded. But I know better. The countdown to New Year's Eve has begun.

48

Jailed Grandson
Trumps Double Arrest

It was a New Year's Eve during one of Bryan's college years. I can't remember which one. After all, we're on year number eight as I write this and the holiday turmoil sometimes runs together. Anyway, it was around midnight and David got a call from Pizza Boy. Both he and Bryan had just gotten arrested for possession of marijuana after being pulled over for a traffic violation.

Wow! I really had Julie now. New Year's Eve. Practically the stroke of midnight and a double arrest. I stopped thinking about what Cindy might be able to contribute on this holiday. I already had more than I thought I'd get tonight. Julie couldn't beat this.

My hopes for winning the crown on this night had been riding on simple drunk driving. Or maybe another family fight, like the time Cindy beat up her mother two days before Thanksgiving. Yet the whole brood still spent the holiday together, all four of them, because no one else in Bucky's family was talking to her. But whoa, a double arrest. This was bonus territory. This would no doubt hit the newspapers and I could add to my Hrablicht Crime Scrapbook. (I still can't believe I changed my legal name. What a dope.)

After David got off the phone and went to the bathroom to attend to his stomach-ache-migraine-anxiety-tremors, I called Julie. It was an hour earlier in Jackson, and I wasn't her only late-night call.

Kerry: Hey Jul, I've got you beat this year. The crown is mine! David just got a call from Pizza Boy. He got pulled over for a traffic violation and the cop searched the car. He and Bryan got arrested for possession of marijuana. Beat that girlfriend!

Julie: (laughing) Sorry Ker, we're now on the second generation. Kevin just got a call from his grandson, Tracy's son. He's in jail.

Kerry: No fucking way! I got two arrests! What are the chances that's gonna happen again? Oh wait, never mind. I can't believe I said that. It'll probably happen next weekend. You win. Geez, how old is he?

Julie: Nineteen.

Kerry: Wow, he's not even a minor. The crown is yours, for now.

Julie: Wait, that's really all we know, that he got arrested. He was on the phone with Kevin, told him he's in jail and then said, "Wait a minute, I gotta call you back." It's been a couple of hours and he still hasn't called back.

Kerry: Okay, let's call it a tie. Happy Fucking New Year.

Julie: Happy Fucking New Year back at you. But hey, what's so *new* about it?

49

The Next Generation Email

Kerry,

Here's some good news about one of Kevin's granddaughters. Judy was the one sent away to a highly disciplined boarding school in Virginia because her father and stepmother couldn't handle her after her mother screwed her up so much. She's doing well and is graduating this May. After much debate, she decided to invite her mother, Trisha, to the ceremony. Trisha told her she couldn't afford to come all the way from Arkansas and stay at a hotel. So the parents of one of Judy's friends said she could stay with them. Great, right? So Trisha called these very nice people and told them she'd be staying for 5 days and bringing her 3 younger children.

Even Judy couldn't believe her nerve. She uninvited her mother. There may be hope for the next generation.

Julie

Hey Julie,

Good to know. Maybe the whole life-sucking-offspring thing works like a recessive gene and skips generations from time to time.

Let's hope. Otherwise you're going to need a scorecard for whatever comes up in the future with all those grandchildren.

Thankfully, I can't imagine any breeding going on in my world.

Kerry

P.S. Tell Judy, "Goot for you!"

50

Moving On

A t 10:30 a.m., the phone rang. David noticed the number on caller
ID and didn't answer it. Cindy left one of her drunken messages
on the machine.

"Hi dad, I'm not drinking or anything," she slurred. "I'm just
calling to tell you something. Something happened. I know Jack won't
tell you but Bryan beat me up again."

We later found out from Jack that this wasn't exactly true. She
wasn't beaten up. But Bryan did slap her around because she brought
home some booze and wanted him to drink with her. He said he was
trying to stay sober so he hit her a few times and walked out.

Cindy's tirade continued on the answering machine.

"Everyone I've talked to, even my therapist, tells me I should
call the police. I don't know what to do," she said.

Perhaps she should have thought about doing what everyone
told her to do, but she never does, so the police didn't get called this
time.

Unfortunately, our phone machine doesn't time out. It just records on and on. So did she.

"Dad, you don't know him. You don't really know what he's like. You give him so much and you don't know what he's really like. He beat me up again. I had to talk to my therapist on the phone because I can't go out looking like this."

Now that's probably true. Over the years, Cindy has gone from being a very pretty girl to looking exactly like what she is, a chain-smoking, overweight drunk. Add some bruises and I can see why she didn't want to go out

She kept slurring about "poor me," but she also had a sisterly concern for Bryan. "Dad, Bryan needs help." That was it, in case you missed it. "You don't know what he's like. Please call me."

All of her messages end with "Please call me." She never leaves a single message. They usually came in threes, building to a crescendo of crying, screaming and threats.

After she hung up from call number one, I asked David to come sit with me so I could keep him calm before the next round. I reminded him that, although she rarely tells the truth, this time we couldn't be sure because it's likely that Bryan beat her up.

He said, "I can't do anything about it." A breakthrough. A real breakthrough.

I said, "That's right. If Bryan really beat her up, she needs to call the police and handle it. Unlike the last time that her mother made her drop the charges and took Bryan in to live with both of them."

About 5 minutes later, she called again and left another message.

"I just wanted to tell you one more thing. If you don't call me back, we have no relationship. I won't talk to you or see you or take money from you." Praise Jesus!!! I put both hands in the air like

Bruce Jenner crossing the finish line of the Olympic decathlon. I knew it would never happen, but for one moment I basked in the glory of possibility.

She continued. "It might as well be like I never existed for you because that's how you treat me now anyway." I guess she forgot all the times he took her drunk calls and told her he would always be there for her when she wasn't drunk. I guess she forgot how he paid for numerous hospitalizations, detox, rehab, school and more. I guess she forgot all the money he recently sent her for her car. I guess she forgot all the times he advised her to get help and get out of her toxic environment. Yep, I guess she forgot.

When she finally stopped talking, David went over to the answering machine, erased both messages and turned it off. He also unplugged the phone. Another breakthrough. He didn't even call Jack to try and confirm anything. I hugged him, told him I was so proud of him, and that this could be a new beginning for us.

Then we both took the dog for a walk. We talked about our taxes, the weather, the dog, golf and more. He talked briefly about how depressed he had been feeling and how he's coming out of it. I reminded him to let go of what he could not control. He said he would and then went on to tell me about his plans to change dentists. Life goes on. Hopefully it will go on without Cindy in it. She's a cancer that can't be cured.

51

The End of the Book

I've had years of practice removing myself from the eye of the storm. I don't let the tornadoes hit me anymore, but when they hit David, I can feel the breeze. I'm on constant clean up duty for my husband in the aftermath, and that has had it's effect on me. Although I love and care deeply about my husband, after 17 years I can honestly say I don't give a shit what happens to any of his kids. They are not worth my time and energy anymore. Outwardly, I know it makes me look like an insensitive bitch to those who haven't witnessed a lifetime of enabling, up close and personal. But walk a mile in my high-heeled shoes and see if you don't become the same jaded, sarcastic, laugh-at-tragedy bitch yourself. It may be the only thing that saves you.

I could have let any one or all of David's tragedies with his children beat me down. But I didn't. Hell, I like kids. I was a teacher. I wanted to save them all, all the kids that came my way. I wanted to believe that I knew what was best for them. But even if I did, they weren't my kids and I had no power, only influence, and not much of that. Interfering and trying to save David's kids, when their parents refused to acknowledge any problems, was futile and almost crippled my marriage. So, as hard as it was, I stepped back. It was like watching a movie. I knew it would end badly, but it was already shot and edited.

My choices were to laugh, cry, or just watch. I started with the crying. Then I moved on to watching. Then I had to laugh at the absurdity of the repetition of events. The repetition of actions. The repetition of reactions.

It pains me to see how much opportunity Jack, Cindy, Bryan, Tracey, Trisha and Terri had, and how they squandered it. They spit in the faces of everyone who tried to help them become better people. Teachers, doctors, therapists, family, friends. Even as adults, when they had moments of clarity and said they would turn their lives around, they never did. They dismissed all real help in favor of wallowing in self-pity, and being supported by daddy's charity and public services. And nothing is ever their fault. They play the blame game and they're in it to win it. I don't get it. How can they live that way when they've had other options?

I listen to talk shows on National Public Radio and hear plenty of research and comments from all over America about social and educational issues. Each time I hear about how poor children are at such a disadvantage, it makes me laugh. If the damn sociologists only knew. If they only got away from their statistics long enough to observe some real, live, rich kids, they'd see some genuinely disadvantaged youth.

Common sense and my own memory tell me that poor people struggle with some things, but overcoming obstacles makes a person stronger. And learning to overcome obstacles makes a person smarter. Kids who don't grow up with a rich father develop survival skills that help them to succeed. They often go on to inspire others to work hard too. Society could use more of "those people."

I've never heard any research on rich kids and how they are at a disadvantage because they enjoy lives of privilege and leisure. No one is looking for problems with children who belong to the country clubs or the Ivy League, so they don't find those problems.

The good schools those rich kids attend aren't labeled as such for the good people they turn out. They're labeled for what's in the building: technology, teacher/student ratio, big shots on the faculty, sports, expansive budgets, test scores.

High grades or family connections can get a kid into Yale or Harvard. But really now, are all the famous graduates good, moral, ethical, hard-working people? All of them? Think now. Many of those graduates are lawyers and politicians, even Presidents. You can do your own jokes.

It's all around us in the media too. Rich families have chauffeurs, maids and ranch hands. The children are catered to. Even the mildly rich kids can be enabled enough to paralyze them for real life. What would become of them if daddy's money ran out? The odds of them making it without an inheritance are not so good in my eyes. I'd rather bet on the kids with acquired skills and life experience.

David and I will be fine. So will Julie and Kevin. Over the years, Julie and I have mellowed and accepted our men as husbands, ignoring the parent part of them. They, in turn, have mellowed and understand that we'll never approve of their child-rearing or adult-enabling methods. They understand how we cope, with humor and each other, and we understand their guilt-driven addiction to fix things with money. It's taken a very long time to arrive at this comfort level.

I've been writing this book for years. Taking notes, turning them into essays, and then chapters. It's gone on for my whole marriage. And it could still go on, if I let it. But I won't. I have come to the conclusion that, although the story won't end, the book must. After all, I have to get the word out. I want to help others choose a different path by letting them see what's on the road ahead if they follow me and Julie. Please don't follow me and Julie. Think of it this way: Julie and I have done this so you don't have to. You can just read about it and live vicariously through us, if you really think you need debilitating chaos in your life.

52

Where Are They Now?

Pizza Boy Jack is now 38 years old and in his 22nd year of delivering pizzas, not all with the same employer, but all in the same area. He's probably a legend. You know, like those teachers whom your parents had and then you had them. He's spanning generations.

He's still a pothead, continues to get food stamps and is on Medicaid for his diabetes drugs. Daddy still pays his rent. When I ask why? David says, "He can't make it on his own." I say, "How will we ever know?"

Jack has gotten to be just as bad an enabler as David, allowing his drunk brother to bounce between his apartment and Bucky's place. And although he claims to despise his mother and sister, he continues to be drawn into their dramas. It probably gives him a sense of being in charge of something.

I haven't encouraged any visits from him in the past few years, so we haven't seen him. David is much better when he keeps his distance and he knows it.

Cindy is 33 and continues to be more of a mess with each passing year. No therapist has ever gotten through to her. So I've got to believe she's just playing them, or they're as jaded and cynical as I am and they've stopped caring. Unethical on their part, but I get it. It's still hard for me to believe that after almost two decades of therapy, she hasn't made *any* changes in her life.

She continues to live with her mother, fight with Bryan and resent Jack. She's unemployed, and although I haven't seen the evidence, I'm sure her mother has her signed up for all kinds of social services.

She has no friends, and her aunts, uncles and cousins don't seem to want to bother with her either.

Bryan, at age 25, is an episode of *Criminal Minds* waiting to happen. Beginning in his senior year of high school, he started writing. Some of it was just scribbling and doodles, but he was consistent with his subject matter. It was all very dark. There were Nazi symbols, violent images of bleeding bodies and stories that debased women. He got some encouragement in his creative writing classes in college, maybe because the professors didn't want to set him off. He definitely has a style, but it's not something a normal person would be comfortable reading. The only comparison I can make is to Truman Capote's *In Cold Blood*, if it were written from the point of view of the murderers, Perry and Dick, with full color illustrations of the Cutter family.

Looking back at all of this makes me wonder if it's the alcohol that did this to him, or if he's truly got something wrong with him that has gone undiagnosed. Whatever it is, he seems to want to stay far away from me and David and only live within the confines of his own little world, inside his brother's or mother's apartment. David and I have stopped expecting him to break free.

Bucky remains an indentured servant to her drunk daughter and a martyr to both her sons. She recently told Jack that she thinks David should come back to Connecticut, get an apartment and live with Bryan. So I guess she feels overwhelmed at times, as she should. I know it's much too late to hope she'll ever end her co-dependency with her children. However, the independent woman in me would like to see her get so fed up that she just takes off and leaves them with no forwarding address. She's had a miserable life since she decided she needed to be free from her marriage. What's it going to take for her to want to break free from her children?

As for Kevin's remaining girls, **Trisha** and **Terry**, not much is known and Julie is very grateful for that. She and Kevin finally have a peaceful life. The girls haven't contacted their mother or father in the past few years. But the fathers of Kevin's grandchildren keep in touch and make sure the kids come to visit. The stepmothers of those grandchildren have also reached out to Kevin and Julie, sometimes for advice. Overall, the children who stay away from their biological mothers are doing fine and the ones who don't, continue to struggle with loyalty issues and more.

When I got to the end of writing this book and called Julie to ask her where the girls are now, she said, "Your guess is as good as mine. I don't know and I don't care!" Once again, it's not the kind of response Julie or I would give about anyone, even a stray dog. But it's the kind of response we had to learn to give *and believe* if we are going to stay sane and married.

Kevin continues to dabble in real estate and other businesses as investments. He also goes on big game hunting trips. Whether he realizes it or not, I'll bet it's therapeutic for him to shoot at stuff.

Julie has embarked on yet another career, this time using her media savvy in politics.

David is still trying to evolve into the carefree retiree he planned on becoming 10 years ago. It's a slow process, but I see progress. He's recently found a hobby in the stock market and still plays enough golf to get his frustrations out by hitting something. He's also an incredible daddy to our dog and two cats. They've had health issues and he is an excellent nursemaid. Of course, he would be, considering the practice he's had.

As for **me**, Kurt Vonnegut said it best, "Laughter and tears are both responses to frustration and exhaustion. I myself prefer to laugh, since there is less cleaning up to do afterward." And this from a guy who didn't even have to deal with mascara.

It took awhile, but I too chose laughter over tears (and insanity) and I wrote it all down. I hope reading it helps someone else.

And now, along with my friend Gail and other women from our writer's club, I'm about to do some public speaking gigs. We're the *Not Dead Yet Girls, Serious Authors, Comic Relief.* We hope our combined wisdom on life's lessons will spark a chuckle or two.

An Invitation to Share

You've probably just had a sigh of relief and said to yourself, "Thank God my life isn't that bad." Well, how bad is it? Really. I want to know.

Are you a second wife or a stepparent who has survived the madness? Do you have any enabling and dysfunctional stories of your own?

I'd love to hear from you. You know, kindred spirits and all that. And believe me, it helps to write out some of your frustrations, re-read them, and laugh. So have at it. I'm here for you.

Website: www.kerrykendall.com

Email: kerry@kerrykendall.com

www.ingramcontent.com/pod-product-compliance
Lightning Source LLC
Chambersburg PA
CBHW060231050426
42448CB00009B/1392